THE CITY
AT EYE LEVEL
IN THE NETHERLANDS

THE CITY AT EYE LEVEL IN THE NETHERLANDS
Published in 2017
Special edition for the Placemaking Week,
Amsterdam, 2017.

PUBLISHER
Uitgeverij Blauwdruk, Wageningen, The Netherlands
www.uitgeverijblauwdruk.nl

PRINTER
Tuijtel, Hardinxveld-Giessendam, The Netherlands
http://www.tuijtel.com

CURATED BY
Jeroen Laven, Sander van der Ham, Siënna Veelders
& Hans Karssenberg
STIPO. Team for urban strategy and city development.
Rotterdam / Amsterdam / Stockholm /Thessaloniki
www.stipo.nl

EDITORS
Wereld in Woorden – Global Research & Reporting,
The Netherlands
Menno Bosma, Edith van Ewijk & Maaike de Hon
www.wereldinwoorden.nl

TRANSLATION
Speer Publications, The Hague, The Netherlands
www.speerpublications.com

GRAPHIC DESIGN
Paola Faoro: Art Direction and Design
Adalberto Camargo: Digital Typesetting

ISBN/EAN 9789492474124

The City at Eye Level is an open source
project.
Visit www.thecityateyelevel.com for:
– Download of the book (pdf) and find more
  chapters, extended versions, and new
  chapters
– Links and backgrounds, and The City at
  Eye Level films
– Great tools and working materials from
  plinths to placemaking
– The network of contributors, and become
  a contributor yourself.

Join our The City at Eye Level Facebook and
Instagram account and become part of the
community, find day to day inspiration, and
share events on the City at Eye Level.

THE CITY
AT EYE LEVEL
IN THE NETHERLANDS

Curated by Jeroen Laven, Sander van der Ham, Siënna Veelders & Hans Karssenberg

CONTENTS

TAKE ACTION NOW

REFLECTIONS

APPENDIX

INTRODUCTION

PREFACE

In early 2012 we launched a project that would become *The City at Eye Level: Lessons for Street Plinths*. In the book, we collected stories from theory and practice about how to ensure that buildings contribute to better public space by maintaining a human scale and a good, active ground floor: the 'plinths' of the building. With our network, we tried to find answers to the question of how to create a good city at eye level. Our work was interdisciplinary and we looked at the physical, the programmatic and the organisational sides of the issue.

Using our own expertise and that of the network, The City at Eye Level quickly became an open source project with dozens of authors all over the world. Indeed, the network expanded thanks to the website www.thecityateyelevel.com, training sessions, lectures and conferences. Collaborative efforts with partners such as the Project for Public Spaces, UN-Habitat, Gehl Architects, cities, developers and many major and minor initiatives from society were a constant source of new inspiration.

The international Placemaking Week in October 2017 in Amsterdam, which we organised with our partners the Project for Public Spaces, Pakhuis de Zwijger, Placemaking Plus and the municipality of Amsterdam was an excellent occasion to put together this book. Welcome to the Netherlands – this book gives a taste of the many things happening right now to improve the quality of public space, maintain a human scale and create more of a sense of place (placemaking).

The Netherlands is a country with a rich tradition in planning. The Dutch economy slowed down in recent years. This had an impact on the development of cities. Parties that traditionally played a pioneering role were given a more modest one. A multitude of new, often smaller parties filled the gap and developed temporary and permanent initiatives to strengthen the cities. There were also parties among the municipalities and developers who came up with new, innovative approaches. Many of these stories, from the Netherlands and from other countries, can be found in the first two City at Eye Level books and on the website. Together these parties have helped to give new impetus for the city. These are open source books and can be downloaded at www.thecityateyelevel.com.

The strengthening of the cities in the Netherlands is continuing unabated. Governments, developers, the large and small new parties who have emerged in recent years, remain active. Challenges and strategies are changing. Many new, small-scale initiatives have entered the arena. The challenge is how to retain and further develop successful initiatives. How can we use them as a foundation for area development and an urban approach aimed at a more human scale and sense of place? How will cities benefit from the rise in construction activity? Will there be space for new initiators, small and large? And how can you effectively manage successful initiatives so that they continue to grow sustainably?

This book compiles examples from medium-sized and large cities in the Netherlands. We have arranged the stories according to the following themes:

– **Introduction:** Overall observations on the city at eye level in the Netherlands. Fred and Ethan Kent, Floris van Alkemade, Charlot Schans, and Hans Karssenberg and Jeroen Laven take us with them.
– **The urban scale:** Journeys on the scale of the city and/or city centre: A new impetus: from Leeuwarden to Maastricht, from The Hague to Doetinchem.
– **Area development:** New approaches to areas covering infrastructure, water and other strategic urban places.
– **Plinths, places and zealous nuts:** Zealous nuts are people with a poor sense of what is apparently impossible, a badge of honour in placemaking. People who make the impossible possible. A number of special projects, from Rotterdam to Amsterdam and from Zaanstad to Gouda.
– **Take action now:** Recent new methods for working on a good city at eye level and their application. From funding to new-build, from sidewalk to picnic.
– **Reflections:** Unifying reflection on the stories in this book by Wouter-Jan Verheul.

STIPO is happy to have the opportunity to work with so many partners on a better city at eye level in the Netherlands and beyond. We work on the ground, analyse and provide training. But we also initiate projects so that we can remain involved in the implementation and management of a good city at eye level.

We hope that this book is a source of inspiration for all those working on cities.

We are extremely grateful to everyone who gave us their time and contributions, which is what made this book possible.

September 2017
Jeroen Laven, Sander van der Ham, Siënna Veelders, Hans Karssenberg

For more inspiration:
- Downloads, articles and methodologies on the city at eye level www. thecityateyelevel.com.
- News, knowledge sharing and community at www.facebook.com/ thecityateyelevel.
- Information about STIPO at www.stipo.nl.
- More background information about the global placemaking movement at www.pps.org.

TOWARDS PLACE-LED DEVELOPMENT IN THE POROUS CITY

Fred Kent, Founder and President Project for Public Spaces & Ethan Kent, Senior Vice President Project for Public Spaces

This book is a labor of love. The exercise of creating it is a very important one, and the lessons learned throughout the process come at an opportune moment given the emerging global conversations on placemaking. We believe the collective narrative will contribute greatly to the interdisciplinary conversations that will take place during Placemaking Week in October 2017 in Amsterdam, The Netherlands.

Last year was the culmination of many global gatherings to make public spaces, streets, public markets, and placemaking a fundamental part of the New Urban Agenda. The final draft of the New Urban Agenda mentions "public spaces" ten times, including the thrust of each of the key messages from the Future of Places conference series.

With Project for Public Spaces' first global Placemaking Week, and our involvement in Habitat III, 2016 saw the Placemaking movement go global. As the conversation turns toward the implementation of the New Urban Agenda, placemaking is being seen as an indispensable tool to bring together the many causes and disciplines necessary to making our cities safer (especially for women and girls), healthier, more sustainable, more resilient, and more just.

The Netherlands is unparalleled in its past success for placemaking, and is now poised to facilitate taking the global placemaking movement to a high level of impact. Often with strong roots in great places in the Netherlands, the Dutch are indeed working around the world to support placemaking. Many local partners of Placemaking Week Amsterdam were also involved in Habitat III, and more recently many helped lead a conference in Nairobi with UN Habitat on implementing the New Urban Agenda through placemaking.

We are inspired by the passionate placemaking processes we've been invited into over the last decade in the Netherlands, and especially by the numerous informal placemaking projects that have recently begun springing up throughout the region. One of the key questions we continue to ask ourselves is how some of these informal placemaking projects and networks, often led by early adopters we affectionately call "zealous nuts," can be supported and scaled up in partnership with governments and developers. How the Netherlands develops successful practices, policies, and implementations, will be central to how "place-led development" can be transferred globally.

More and more, placemaking has been occurring "upside down": starting with *places* and *people*, with more small scale, low cost, informal interventions. However, the impact is often limited. A real challenge and opportunity is to figure out how these interventions can

also really "turn upside down" the way we participate in cities, the way we finance transitions, the way we do larger designs and think about goverance structure.

The big question is how we also scale up *the impact* of place making? How can we build on the successes of momentum for "lighter, quicker, cheaper" interventions? How do these developments attract people, investment, and developers on the terms of these communities? They are going to be developed one way or another, but how do we really achieve place-led inclusive development?

Placemaking should not be dominated by any one sector: successful placemaking is balanced between different sectors. There is room for leadership in several sectors and contexts; government, communities and private sector. In every part of the world one sector helps to lead placemaking, and we have to learn from that, as this leading sector often also is the most innovating. For example, in Australia and New Zealand, governments are progressive and they are doing a pretty good job. However, there is less leadership from philanthropy and community-based organizations. It is still government doing *for* others and not so much *with* them. Different phases of projects will bring about different tensions and the question is how governments can find a balance between the interests of all parties. One of the key lessons is that while communities certainly have the ability and knowledge necessary for effective placemaking processes, they often simply don't have the capacity to do it on their own, without the help of local government, partners, and allies.

The placemaking process is a way to bring different actors together in a constructive, collaborative way, to draw on more resources, ideas, and creativity for shaping places. Placemaking is about engaging, challenging, and empowering, everyone to help shape the public realm, and subsequently their city, and their local economy. To do this we need to make everything about cities more open and porous, from the plinth and eye-level, to the planning process, to the access to resources for starting businesses and upward mobility, to governance. Not only will this make a better, more inclusive, and loved city, it will build the capacity of cities to take on any challenge.

There are great opportunities for growing models for scaling up and sustaining placemaking efforts. How do we develop place-led governance, financing, and design, that can scale up and how do we sustain the upside-down planning?

We strongly feel that it is through networks that these models are going to emerge and be best applied. There is so much learning to do and we need to make change happen faster by learning from and creating feedback loops. In the last five years, we have been creating a collective impact model with the Placemaking Leadership Council.

We have a network of over 1500 people right now and it is being broken down into groups of people focusing on regional efforts, citywide or national efforts, but also on crosscutting issues.

We need everyone to ask more, and bigger, questions and to realize that it is never one discipline's job to do placemaking alone. How can we engage and challenge everybody to be part of placemaking. We all have to show more leadership and responsibility. That's also where the new models of place governance come in.

We really appreciate the great generosity of the Netherlands, its cities and people, in sharing what they are learning themselves. This book presents numerous case studies whereby people have been remarkably open in their successes and struggles. We also appreciate the generosity STIPO has offered with creating this book, hosting the conference together with The City at Eye Level, Placemaking Plus and Pakhuis de Zwijger. We are very lucky to benefit from the openness the Netherlands is offering to us, and placemakers everywhere to learn from each-other and work together. We are confident that this event will create a foundation for us to collectively realize our potential to implement placemaking globally.

WE MUST REDEFINE PUBLIC SPACE

Chief government architect Floris Alkemade

Chief government architect Floris Alkemade provides advice – solicited or unsolicited – about the architecture and urban environment of state property. He was trained as an architect and has a wealth of experience here and abroad. Our conversation with him is about the dynamics of public space, new opportunities that have arisen as a result of the demise of shopping streets and the question of whether it's really necessary for it to be so lively everywhere in our Dutch cities.

How do you view the development of public space in the Netherlands?
'Public space is in constant flux. Right now, the survival of many shopping spaces is under threat. That begs the question of how to design inner city public space without all of these shops. It's tricky, but it also opens up new possibilities. I view this continuous focus on shopping as the dominant activity as an impoverishment of what public space could be. It's not per se a bad culture, but the major risk is that public space will be designed solely with consumption in mind, and that's what will cause this widespread impoverishment. Another intriguing thing about our generation is this almost obsessive need for conviviality. It has to "lively" everywhere: busy, but not too busy either. Why actually? To what extent is that a realistic expectation? You can also have beautiful spaces with a certain tranquillity, where nothing is being sold.'

What's the secret of good public space?
'Look at urban spaces, at well-functioning squares. Look at the size, the programming and particularly at the boundaries, the walls around the square.

Good proportions in public space are often decisive factors. Lange Voorhout in The Hague illustrates this well. It's one of the most beautiful urban spaces that I know. There are roads running through it, cars are parked there and there are very few shops or public programmes. But the space, the proportions, they simply work. It's a space where you're happy to spend more time than you had anticipated. One of the decisive factors is that the promenade, the act of walking, is the main focus. The main route is in the middle.'

What are specific characteristics of Dutch cities and what challenges do they face?
'I just got back from China. The density of the new cities is huge there, as a result of which there are a lot of people walking on the street and so many more amenities too. That's an enormous impetus for public life. Low density is typically Dutch. How can you liven up public space without density, without this pressure? I do have hope because I've noticed that more and more attention is being devoted to how public space is designed in the Netherlands. There is a great deal of appreciation for the intelligence embedded in the old structures and an awareness of the importance of the inner city. But at the same time this structure is also vulnerable. Two or three apathetic projects is all it takes to ruin magnificent streets. Not everyone is aware of this vulnerability. I've been to many American cities. When you get out of your car there, you

sometimes have no idea how to experience the city as a pedestrian any more: you simply can't walk to anything. Everything is oriented towards the car. It's always a relief to walk down the street in the Netherlands again and realise how generous and self-evident the public space has been designed here.'

Are Dutch cities capable of raising the bar in terms of quality?
'Suddenly there are many vacant shops in medium-sized cities, especially in the provincial cities. That gives the impression of decline and bankruptcy, which is hard to swallow. Every change is difficult, but the collapse of all of these shops is an extremely fundamental change that really requires the input of municipalities' design strength. Indeed, the new environmental and planning vision asks municipalities to describe environmental qualities. That's also important for developers. The primary concern for them is concrete projects and making a profit, but they're often highly capable of investing more if they know that they're operating in a context with clear future value. It's the responsibility of lower levels of government to create a clear picture of where they're going. I hope that municipalities will be able to use their design strength in the right way. Many cities don't have an urban planning service of any importance anymore. There's a danger that some cities start to lose their grip, but that can be overcome by involving good designers in the development of environmental and planning visions.'

Are there any notable examples?
'It's exciting to see how the most impossible places can still start a new life. Wibautstraat in Amsterdam has improved immensely following renovations, particularly the Volkshotel. Your main thought there in the past was 'how do I get out of here as quickly as possible?' Strijp-S in Eindhoven is another interesting area where all kinds of little companies are popping up. It's precisely that kind of inappropriateness about the buildings there that has led to alternative uses. The 'Haagse loper', the pedestrian boulevard running from Central Station to the ministries and the city hall, has been given a major overhaul. It's also about having to build awareness and a culture. That comes in waves. For example, the development of waterfronts is a fairly recent phenomenon. Even the idea that water is something attractive is relatively recent. Not surprisingly, because the water used to stink much more. I find that interesting, the transience of what seems a given.'

What are the key challenges for the future?
'If you were to the reports about the meteoritic rise of self-driving cars seriously, then we certainly won't be driving less in the future, but there will be fewer privately owned cars. The impact of that will be huge. If you can picture our residential streets and squares with 25% fewer parking places, then you can imagine what kind of fantastic opportunities that will generate. More space will become available for a different use of these places, which will only improve the quality.

'In addition, society is ageing rapidly. On top of that, care is being organised in institutes increasingly infrequently, and people are living at home longer. The question is whether that has something meaningful to offer the quality and design of public space. We have to stop seeing ageing exclusively as a problem. If we design public space effectively for the elderly, then ageing could be a fantastic impetus for public life in our cities and villages.

'Another important function of public space is that people meet each other. You mustn't underestimate that. Sports, work, schools are all segregated and groups of people are being increasingly disassociated. Everywhere you look, everything is being screened off. It's the task of the government and other parties working on the city to be alert to that and ensure that we don't systematically shut out groups.'

How do you hope that we go into the next 20 years?
'That we treat the public domain as an independent assignment that requires as much attention as any other building project. A building project receives planning, a budget and programming. Do the same for the public domain and don't view it as leftover space. We can make beautiful space with good designing. Of course you have to programme functions, but make sure that you can maintain the quality once these functions are no longer there. Dutch inner cities are places that are worked on generation by generation. So there's an opportunity there to improve all that has been placed there in the past: keep what's worth keeping and don't be shy to change things. That's what improves cities.'

PLACEMAKING HAS TO GO BEYOND BEING TEMPORARY

Charlot Schans is programme maker at Pakhuis De Zwijger, platform for creation and innovation in Amsterdam, which is co-organising and hosting the Placemaking Week. Schans focuses primarily on urban development and social innovation.

Charlot, what do you want to convey at the Placemaking Week?
'That placemaking, when properly implemented, is an interesting tool to bring together stakeholders, including the less obvious ones, based on a shared ambition. The fact that it's about improving *public* space makes it easier to experiment with a co-creative approach than it would if you were refurbishing a building together, for example. Placemaking doesn't mean quickly throwing together a public-private partnership. Rather, it's a complex process that involves crafting a level playing field that controls for the latitude and leverage of stakeholders. The public space is the first thing you experience there. I'm always inspired by examples that break out of their own mould, that operate on the interface of the public and the private, and that provide an area with added value; initiatives that, in addition to public space, also generate housing and workspace, and that are driven by principles such as circularity and co-creation.'

Why is Pakhuis De Zwijger involved in the Placemaking Week?
'Liveable cities that are welcoming and sustainable excite us. It's unique to have a group of people together who are engaged with that

at the global level. At Pakhuis de Zwijger we organise daily meetings
to think about and work on solutions with stakeholders from the city.
Many mistakes were made here in the past, so the more dialogue and
inspiration, the better.'

What kind of mistakes?
'Soulless new-build that doesn't consider the use of public space and
neglects the plinths. The IJburg district is a good example of that. Too
little thought still goes into a good mixture of functions. The result is
dull residential neighbourhoods and industrial estates.'

**Do you mainly play a facilitating role or do you also help to set the
agenda?**
'Both. But sometimes I would like to play a bigger role in agenda-
setting. We work a lot with developers and municipalities. Process
innovation doesn't come naturally to many of these parties.'

What's your opinion of placemaking in the Netherlands?
'We tend to think that things are better elsewhere, but I think the level
of urban planning in the Netherlands is reasonably high, especially
when it comes to involving stakeholders. If you compare that to how
things work in cities like Bucharest... You realise that the polder
model, the idea that we have to do things together, is in our blood.'

**You're closely involved in the city makers movement. Tell us a bit
about that.**
'In recent years, Pakhuis de Zwijger has established networks in
cities in the Netherlands and Europe in order to share inspiration
and knowledge. City makers are usually citizen-driven initiatives,

in which residents, for example, take action against vacancy or set up an energy cooperative together. These initiatives have been popping up all over the place in recent years, partly as a consequence of the economic crisis, which stopped many commercial projects in their tracks and created room for bottom-up initiatives. In Amsterdam, De Ceuvel (a circular art factory in the north of Amsterdam, ed.) and Roest (an urban oasis in the east of Amsterdam, ed.) are good examples of that, as is Holzmarkt in Berlin. The latter project is more activist than De Ceuvel. A referendum managed to stop office development along the Spree river. Subsequently, an urban village 18,000 square metres large was created there, including housing and studios, a park, a club, a hotel, stages… Aside from making clever use of the creativity of its supporters, Holzmarkt also succeeded in securing financing from pension funds and private sources, which I think is impressive. What I've noticed is that projects that know how to articulate their added value effectively have managed to successfully negotiate about gaining permanent status. Another characteristic is that they're effective at establishing a connection between what's happening inside and outside, by also taking care of the public space.'

What are the characteristics of the city makers movement?
'It's a many-headed beast, but then in a positive sense. It's an extremely broad movement. It covers hyper-local and volunteering to highly entrepreneurial. Now that the economy of most cities is picking up again, it's time to take the next step. Otherwise it will be business as usual again before you know it, in which the highest bidder wins, and then the movement will be wiped off the map as quickly as it appeared.'

What is this next step?
'To go beyond the temporary. We have to start thinking about ownership and creating a level playing field in which all stakeholders join the discussion as equal partners. If you want permanent status, you have to give it serious thought in advance. That entails making a baseline measurement and thinking about your value proposition and governance.'

What's a good example of that?
'Hotel Buiten on Sloterplas. What they've managed to do there is connect the reinvigoration of Sloterplas with the municipality's goal of spreading the public more across the city. I believe that knowing how to effectively communicate "what's in it for us", and so not just for you, is a hallmark of professionalization. If you're unable to do that, to communicate the broader aim and capitalise on it, then you'll notice the energy ebbing away after five or seven years. Because by then the spirit to do all of this volunteer work will

have vanished and a broader base will be needed. Sometimes projects don't have enough professionalism in their nature and need guidance. But then they're confronted by the fact that there really isn't anyone out there who can help. Yes, sometimes public servants help on a private basis, but they soon end up playing dual role. STIPO is an agency that could take on that role, just as we could.'

How are developers and the municipalities dealing with placemaking?
'Municipalities face a huge construction task and may become less innovative as a result. Process innovation is in danger of succumbing again as a result of the increased speed of building, whereas the quality of life and public space should be included as conditions during the tender phase. I'm seeing more exciting things happening with developers at the moment. AM, for example, is building for specific target groups, such as millennials, and is devoting attention to the environment and plinths as well. And BPD is experimenting with a shared plinth, in which the entire neighbourhood is responsible for its allocation and operation.'

Should there be more De Ceuvels?
'Of course, that would be great. But if that's not feasible at the plot level; then I'd like to see elements of it integrated into other projects. The value of these kinds of creative and vibrant places is increasingly being recognised. The fact that Roest is receiving a permanent place in the development of Oostenburgereiland is evidence of that. The Westerdokmodel (which stipulates that new construction projects should make temporary, affordable art factories available, ed.) is a positive development. But it's a shame that it was a temporary incentive there, and now there are mainly lawyers' offices there. Art factories should be an enduring part of new neighbourhoods. But that doesn't always happen because Amsterdam is still too often driven by short-term financial motives. Luckily, people are experimenting more, as is the case with the mercantile development area N-kavel in Sloterdijk.'

What lessons can we learn from other countries?
'Mainly that other types of financing and organisational models exist. For example, it's easier to start up a cooperative in Germany: this legal form is more common there. I've also noticed that there's more leeway regarding decision-making in many other countries. Administrators simply say: I think you're great, welcome aboard. In the Netherlands, decision-making is more watertight. I'm in favour of zones with fewer regulations.'

What is the Netherlands doing right?
'It's easier to get your alderman on the phone here. We are riding on an activist past. There's constructive dialogue. Whereas some European countries are still completely focused on democratisation, here there's a post-activist vibe in the air. There's a constant urge to talk to each other.'

You've been engaging in placemaking yourselves by claiming the square in front of your premises...

'Yes, we did that in 2016 on the occasion of our tenth anniversary. We called it City Makers Square. That's what Google Maps calls It. Piet Heinkade, where we are located, was supposed to become a lively boulevard, but instead became a windy avenue of offices. We claimed the square to wake people up: do something with your environment! Public servants come here every day, but they've never uttered a word about it.'

DO:

– Do it together. View placemaking as a process. The ownership, the governance and the funding should be properly arranged.

DON'T:

– Don't view placemaking as something temporary. Don't see it as a bottom-up or a top-down process: it's both simultaneously. And don't see placemakers as a tool for creating property value.

PUBLIC SPACE AND PLACEMAKING IN NL

From experimental to standard practice, Hans
Karssenberg & Jeroen Laven (STIPO)

To call the Netherlands the Mecca of placemaking is perhaps a bit of
an exaggeration, but compared to most countries we do have a head
start in terms of urban development and the quality of public space.
That's partly because urbanisation occurred early in the Netherlands:
80% of the population already lived in urban areas by the eighteenth
century. The human dimension has always been a characteristic
feature of these early cities, as is evident from the intimate streets
and places, designed with the pedestrian in mind. The Dutch 'stoep',
or sidewalk, that emerged at the time as a buffer between public and
private space even became an 'export product'. The stairs in New York
are derived from it and named after it: 'stoep' (see chapter about the
Sidewalk on page 218).

Cities are based on a mixture of quality of life, housing and work.
Hotels, cafés, homes, shops – everything is mixed together. While
splendid squares were built in Italy and Spain to honour and glorify the
nobility and the Church, the historic squares here reflected the Dutch
entrepreneurial spirit and were mostly markets. An excellent example
is the origin of Dam Square in Amsterdam. Initially, the Nieuwe Kerk
was supposed to dominate the square, but as the design phase
approached, trade routes to the East gained importance and the city
hall became increasingly powerful. In the final design, the city hall,
now the palace on Dam Square, pushed the church to the background.
That's typical of the history of the development of the city.

STRONG PLANNING TRADITION

In the 1930s, urban development in the Netherlands grew significantly. For the first time, large areas were developed in one go, thus creating a complete public space. That's fairly unique in the world. Urban designers worldwide still visit Amsterdam to look at H.P. Berlage's South Plan. For Berlage, the quality of the public space was the nerve centre of his design. Streets and spaces came first, and only then the buildings. He thus introduced a fantastic urban system, highly flexible, and with public space as the backbone.

After the Second World War, the Netherlands built a strong tradition in planning, which is based on the CIAM notion of the 'functional city'. The *Congrès Internationaux d'Architecture Moderne* (1928-1959), led by Le Corbusier and other modernists, advocated a more rational urban planning with separate functions. Planning became functional. One positive effect of that, for example, is the relatively limited gentrification in Dutch cities thanks to strong social housing associations. It's also responsible for the high level of traffic safety for pedestrians and cyclists. The fact that people make excursions to Dutch cities to see how space has been allocated for bicycles shows how unique the latter is. Incidentally, the government only prioritised bicycles over cars in the 1970s after social pressure from the 'Stop killing our children' campaign.

And yet somewhere something went wrong. Indeed, the negative side of the planning system is that it's extremely rational and does exactly the opposite of what Berlage was doing: it first plans all the functions and only looks at public space at the end. As a result, many soulless, monotonous residential areas were built with poor quality public space.

From the 1970s the system also focused strongly on people moving out of the cities. In the meantime, cars were taking over the city centres. It's hard to imagine today, but Nieuwmarkt Square in Amsterdam was populated by cars, as were many other squares in the Netherlands.

FROM FORMAL TO INFORMAL

In the 1990s, people's need to meet and interact grew, and user experience became increasingly important. Pedestrians began to reconquer the city from cars; more outdoor cafés and places where people can meet started to appear. An interesting tension arose between formal and informal. People living in rigid systems found a way to give themselves some air by building a small garden in front of their façade or putting a bench next to the door. The government condoned this and even helped to remove the first stone from the

wall: the formal embraces the informal. Thus a hybrid zone
was created with an extremely important social function: 80%
of informal contact between neighbours takes place there
(see The Sidewalk, page 218).

Cities became popular places again and there was a huge need for
housing. Prior to the recent crisis, the construction industry focused
on standardising as much as possible so that there was as little left
for them to do as possible on construction sites. That goes against
the grain of prioritising the human dimension. Forced by the crisis,
the construction industry had to focus on reusing existing buildings,
and in such cases standardisation is difficult. In the meantime, many
bottom-up initiatives appeared, also for improving public space.

The general feeling in the Netherlands now, as you will read in this
book, is that the crisis is over. It will be exciting for cities to see how
they will manage to keep working on the quality of their public space.
As a result of developments in recent decades, the Netherlands faces
the challenge of connecting a strong, rational and functional planning
tradition with the other half of the brain: the user experience, the city
at eye level. Users don't only need space, they also need experiential
value. People don't only want to reside, they also want to experience
something their environment. Essentially there's nothing wrong with
the rational tradition, as long as it's not the only one. The modernists

made the error of wanting to capture the city in rational models. That can't be done. You also have to use intuition, norms and values, and social structures in your design.

THE ECONOMY OF THE PEDESTRIAN

A number of developments are providing opportunities to connect these both of these sides of the brain. One of these is the rise of the pedestrian, which is related to the economic transition from production to creativity and knowledge to innovation and 'meeting up'. Despite all of the internet and other communication options, innovation moves the fastest when people are within walking distance of each other and their opportunities to exchange. So these have to be pleasant places to stay. The quality of these places, that's what it's all about.

As a result of this, the economy of the pedestrian is become more important than that of the motorist. It's about walking, meeting, experiencing and no longer about making things as easy as possible with the car. Research by the Brookings Institution argues that we should no longer think in terms of kilometres but in terms of steps. That's the major challenge, because cities know everything about the car, at any given moment of the day, but in most cases they don't know anything about pedestrians. If the economy of the pedestrian is to really become increasingly important, then we need to conduct research on where pedestrians walk, what they do and when, but also on their experiences and emotions.

Some cities are already working on this issue. For example, Amsterdam has its first plan for pedestrians, and Rotterdam is the first city in the world to develop a plinth strategy, which primarily benefits the pedestrian.

The Netherlands is thus responding to an international trend. All over the world, people are rediscovering the existing city and prioritising the pedestrian. Almost every city in the Netherlands is itching to get started, which is evident in essentially every chapter of this book.

CITYWIDE PLACEMAKING

The 'two halves of the brain' approach is about how to combine reason and emotion. As a human being, what do you want to experience in the city? What do you want to be able to do in your residential neighbourhood? User experience is about meeting other people. Zomerhofkwartier (ZOHO) in Rotterdam is a great example of the transition from 'space to place'. This project was driven by a combination of top-down and bottom–up initiatives that mobilised the community's networks and allowed for surprises to happen.

People start to appropriate space, and then suddenly a chef comes by and says: I want to start a restaurant in that old train. He starts growing vegetables and installs an outdoor café. The place becomes a little paradise where people like to be.

We now have to move towards citywide placemaking. ZOHO and other similar places evolved as an experiment, but it's important to encourage this kind of development in other places in the city. Take street markets, for example. The Netherlands has a strong tradition in that respect, but the markets are doing poorly at the moment. That's because they're purely seen as places to buy and sell. But a market can be so much more: a place where users can experience the neighbourhood, meet people and buy healthy food, and a place where local entrepreneurs can build a small-scale economy. It's already happening here and there, but industry should think hard now about how to strengthen and use the traditional markets as a way of creating places.

And that's true of so many issues related to placemaking. Think, for example, of water in the city: there are few places where people can actually access it, and that's a pity. In Amsterdam, for example, they've cleaned the canals so thoroughly that you can even swim in them now.

How can we change that in other places too? In short, we have to move from an accumulation of experiments to a citywide placemaking approach.

FROM PLACEMAKING TO PLACE MANAGEMENT

That means working on placemaking in areas for several years on end. It means forming coalitions and finding financial resources for these areas. The condition for making the transition from placemaking to place management is that we give users of the city who come up with initiatives access to the strong planning system. But how do you adapt this kind of system to the necessity of making of exceptions? Think, for example, of management and enforcement. In the Netherlands, everything's clean, intact and safe, but we don't concern ourselves with whether things are also social, fun and comfortable. We need to also extend management to the two halves of the brain and ensure that solutions can be customised. But how do you achieve that? A service that manages 125,000 kilometres of asphalt and 1,000 bridges will say: you're crazy if you intend to make exceptions for everything. It's an interesting challenge: how can we work together with these kinds of systems?

We also need to look at the sustainability of placemaking. Many initiatives succeed in breathing new life into a place, but after a few years the energy ebbs away and they collapse.

If you want people to continue to do things, you have to reward their efforts by giving them influence. How do you organise that? A developer shouldn't only work on buildings. That means a whole new way of working in which you have to look carefully at the question: who lives and works there, and what are they doing with the area? When we organise meetings with the public, the people that show up are usually white males above the age of 55. We need to address the groups that aren't showing up and aren't being reached by us.

By and large, this isn't about creating but about enticing. And about finding a structural basis, so that people have a lasting role. It's much easier for a municipality to subsidise a project than adapt the system, but the latter is the challenge that we're faced with right now. It's quite a task, but luckily everyone can tap into what's already happening. A kind of toolbox has been created in this country, which can be used by all of these cities, professionals and bottom-up initiators. That's what this book is about. That's why we close this chapter with five models that we have seen emerge. So that together we can seize the momentum.

The temporary use of both vacant properties and poorly used outdoor space is extremely important to strengthen neighbourhoods and streets. We need to sit down with stakeholders and figure out which function can be added to improve the entire street. If we don't do that and rent out vacant buildings for a low price, the neighbours will start to rebel. But if you install cafés and restaurants in consultation with shopkeepers, for example, in order to attract more people, or add a sewing or knitting shop in a fashion street, no one will object. That's also true of urban farming on desolate plots. These are initiatives with an incredibly positive spin-off, which not only improve cohesion in the neighbourhood, but also health.

One of the most beautiful examples of how temporary use can help to develop a neighbourhood is the Westerdok art factory. This new-build neighbourhood in Amsterdam was constructed about ten years ago. The plinths often have trouble getting off the ground in new neighbourhoods. So we asked ourselves how we can make this neighbourhood part of the city. A number of plinths were offered at low rent for creative pursuits such as a cooking studio and an architecture firm. They were told that as long as they made a concerted effort to breathe new life into this neighbourhood, they could sign a ten-year lease. Everything in this neighbourhood fell right into place from day one.

2 STREET MANAGEMENT

A successful example of street management is a street called Meent in Rotterdam. Real estate investor Robin von Weiler noticed that the shopping street was deteriorating, so he mobilised all of the owners to develop a joint strategy. At its core was diversification: a focus on quality and small shops manned by the owners themselves. Moreover, Von Weiler had his hand in everything: he made sure that the employment agency was moved so that the closed plinths could be opened up, the layout of the street changed, the lampposts, everything. Within a few years, Meent has become one of the most popular shopping streets in Rotterdam.

Another example of a street that made a complete U-turn is in the Klarendal area in Arnhem. Klarendaalseweg, which was once populated by bakeries and butchers, became completely vacant after the war. Drug dealing and prostitution took over the area. One day, the residents were fed up with it all and chased out the drug lords. The housing association bought up, renovated and prepared the retail premises for new use. They decided, together with Artis, the country's top fashion institute, to offer the buildings to graduates. The ex-students paid normal rent, but what they got in return was a studio on the street where they could work and which they were obliged to open to the public. There are now 50 fashion designers on Klarendaalseweg, and Arnhem has become a fashion city.

3 PLACE MANAGEMENT

Bryant Park in New York is a source of inspiration when it comes to public-private partnerships. Forty years ago, this was a no-go area. All of the area's stakeholders got together at the time and asked themselves: what can we do to make the park a better space, a better place. Subsequently, an organisation was hired to take full responsibility of both the physical management and the programming. In the meantime, there are outdoor cafés, a ping pong table, high-quality green areas and a variety of events taking place in the park. The budget is US$10 million a year and is partly financed by property owners who understand that this is an intelligent investment, because it stands to raise the value of their real estate. The restaurants

also contribute part of their profit. An extensive model has been developed here that's extremely sustainable. For 40 years now they've been experimenting on how best to do things. They're already working on their third generation of kiosks because they weren't happy with the first two, and so they are constantly trying out things and continuing to develop. Bryant Park illustrates well why things should never be a one-off but should have structural permanence, and consequently why it's important to form coalitions and guarantee cash flows. Inspired by this model, we recently set up a similar place management organisation in Rhijnhuizen (see the chapter on it on page 126).

No matter what kind of placemaking you introduce, it will have an impact on the entire area. One of the most important lessons that we learned from the developments at Zomerhofkwartier is that we forgot to think about funding in advance. The fight against vacancy and efforts to improve the area have rapidly increased the value of the real estate there. If we had agreed on a deal three years ago to share the difference between the value now and the value then, then we would have an organisation with a budget that would allow it to work a long time in the area. In new areas, we try to incorporate that idea immediately now, so that the partners that benefit from returns can reinvest them. There are already some good examples of how that works in practice. Such as Zuidas in Amsterdam, where Saskia Rill is a plinth manager (see also the chapter about Zuidas on page 92). One half of her salary is paid by the municipality, and the other half is paid by all of the owners in the area.

Erasmusveld in The Hague (see the chapter on it on page 120) is also an excellent example of area management. The municipality wants a highly sustainable neighbourhood to be developed there. Together with other stakeholders, area developer BPD Ontwikkeling is constructing a city garden there and a tiny houses village in order to give the area that they're going to develop in the future a different identity. They involve the community in what they're doing and aren't only focusing on the higher income parts of the area, but also on existing adjacent neighbourhoods.

Many cities have embraced a 'city at eye level' strategy at the city or inner city level. Rotterdam is doing it with its City Lounge strategy; Groningen as a cycling city already started doing it in the 1970s; Leeuwarden took on the role of cultural capital and said: we're no longer looking at the places but at the whole city, and we're handing over responsibility to the 'mienskip', the community. Maastricht has actually been doing it for decades simply by making nice places. Having managed to make the massive shift from a city for cars to a city for slow traffic, Maastricht is creating large public spaces that are much more attractive for pedestrians. In addition the city is trying to create conditions to ensure that these spaces are used well. Driven by its urban strategy, the city is truly thinking about how

to eventually ensure that it creates good places with attention to every detail. Instead of forcing it on small places and then moving on to the larger places, Maastricht is going from large to small. In Tilburg, in addition to redesigning Spoorzone, the municipality is also examining how to make the city centre more closely knit, so that it becomes an appealing city to spend time in. A little along the lines of how that transpired in Melbourne. Essentially it's happening all over the country.

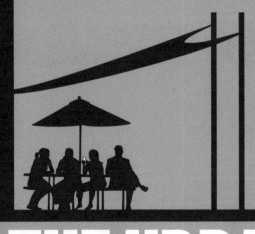

THE URBAN

SCALE

PLACEMAKING + FRIESLAND = MIENSKIP

Does a province that has its own language also have its own form of placemaking? You bet! 'For us, placemaking is always about mienskip', says Harmen de Haas, director of urban planning and administration in the municipality of Leeuwarden. Many dictionaries give 'community' as a synonym for the word 'mienskip', but Haas views it as a much broader concept. 'It means being conscious of your own culture and everyone pitching in as a team, whereby people take responsibility for their actions. Our role as the municipality is to bring people together. We view the city as a campus, and we're building it together.'

For the Frisian capital that means never focusing solely on the city anymore. 'These days, the emphasis in urban development is often on big cities. But smaller and medium-sized cities, such as Leeuwarden, are fundamentally different. We have a strong link to our rural areas. We feel responsible for them and depend on them, and we emphasise that in placemaking too.'

A second fundamental element in Frisian-style placemaking is fluidity – which De Haas believes is directly linked to the geography of Friesland. 'Everyone here lives near water,' he says. Fluid placemaking means that projects aren't rigid but rather are open to outside influences.

A third aspect of placemaking in Friesland is that 'places of hope' are being created. De Haas interprets that as 'giving desire a place'.

These elements are evident in the plans that Leeuwarden is developing for 2018, the year in which the city will be cultural capital of Europe. Leeuwarden-Fryslân 2018 (LF2018) won this desirable status with a bid under the heading 'iepen mienskip' ('iepen' means 'open').

Being the cultural capital of Europe presents many opportunities, according to De Haas. 'Among other things, it acts as an accelerator. There's a deadline with a limited amount of preparation time, which creates a sense of urgency. It also leads to a rethink and speeds up the development of projects.'

An example of the projects that De Haas is referring to is the approach of the Oldehoofsterkerkhof, the large square in the centre of Leeuwarden, where the town is situated, among other things. 'There are all kinds of institutes there working with language. Their front doors are shut. We want to open these doors with the LF2018 event Lân fan Taal (Country of Language), by means of both physical measures, such as language pavilions, and programming about multilingualism. And mienskip plays an emphatic part in this programming.'

One of the language pavilions is the TaalExpo. The aim of this expressive construction is to enliven the Oldehoofsterkerkhof the entire year round and act as a grandstand during events that already frequently take place on weekends.

Another example are the sculptures of Spanish artist Jaume Plensa. The municipality wanted to reinvigorate the station area. The initial idea was to install a fountain there. But Plensa didn't think it was a good idea to have a fountain in a city with Leeuwarden's climate. He preferred images surrounded by mist. He believes that they complement typical Leeuwarden institutions, such as the renowned international water technology institute Wetsus, which is located near the station on the ancient urban river Potmarge.

The inhabitants of Leeuwarden welcomed Plensa's idea. The only people who had objections were traffic engineers and urban planners. 'More than anything,' De Haas says, 'I think they need to get used to the new way of working. But we persevered with the sculptures, and ultimately they helped us to make it possible. The traffic engineers and urban planners could be a little less dominant though.'

The new way of working that De Haas is referring to prioritises 'inviting'. 'We're good at that as a municipality. We believe that we need to engage with the different parties, parties that have the drive to improve the city and province. We take the initiative and invite people to come up with ideas. But if they do approach us, then they have to be willing to take action. In fact, we always ask them: are you here on your own or on behalf of something else? Ideas have to be a part of the mienskip. So if you have a plan, you have to mobilise support yourself.'

The Frisians have a long tradition of cooperation, though that way of working is sometimes perceived to be slow-going. De Haas acknowledges that decision-making sometimes goes at a snail's pace, or as the Frisian's say 'op zijn elfendertigst' (at eleven and thirty). This expression can be directly traced back to Friesland. Apparently it refers to the slow manner in which the States of Frisia, consisting of representatives from 11 cities and 30 'grietenijen' (the administrative districts of the public prosecutors), deliberated. 'The drawback of relying on cooperation is that sometimes it doesn't go beyond business as usual,' De Haas adds. 'We've been breaking with that here and there in recent years, because the will is there.'

The municipality is trying to move away from the custom of arranging everything formally. It is deliberately relaxing regulations. Art and culture are playing a remarkably important role. When Leeuwarden develops a new area on the outskirts of the city, the municipality will first give it a temporary use, in the form of theatre or music, for example. Art also serves as an alternative for expensive urban development interventions. The artist Giny Vos reinvigorated an alley, for example, by hanging the skeleton of a whale over it equipped with LED lighting.

One part of mienskip is that the authorities create space for people. As an example, De Haas cites the cooperation with shopkeepers. 'They often claim public space, because it's part of their display window. Authorities are quick to think: we have to intervene. We're doing things differently, however. We let the shopkeepers arrange and rectify matters. One is example is when they put benches down somewhere to liven up the street. We give them that space. Because you can easily mess up the mienskip by acting strictly.'

Another example of mienskip, in which Leeuwarden and its surroundings figure prominently, is the Kening fan 'e Greide (King of the Meadows) project. Its aim is to preserve the quality of the landscape. Scientists, farmers, musicians, communication people and others are working together on this project. Using the black-tailed godwit as its symbol, the project addresses major issues regarding 'landschapspijn' (a newly coined phrase meaning 'landscape pain'), biodiversity and nature-inclusive agriculture in such a way that it also affects the city and its inhabitants. The project recently won the Anita Andriesen Award for spatial quality for having brought attention to 'the discussion about the quality of the landscape in Friesland and beyond'.

DO:
– Ask yourself how large the group is that is working on a plan; don't act on individual wishes and hobbyists. Give people a chance. Try out things and have the courage to conclude that you're on the wrong path and need to make adjustments. You learn from that.

DON'TS:
– Don't lay down everything in rules in advance, because that will only lead to failure.
– Don't jump into projects too quickly, that can cost money.

DRECHTSTEDEN: WORKING ON A DRIERIVIERENPUNT WITH NO INTERNAL BORDERS

Three rivers – the Beneden-Merwede, the Oude Maas and the Noord – converge at a point in South Holland, aptly named Drierivierenpunt, or the Three River Junction. In fact, it's the busiest river junction in Europe. Three municipalities are located at this junction: Dordrecht, Papendrecht and Zwijndrecht. The individual city maps of these cities stop where the water begins: in other words, the maps don't show what's on the other side of the water. Thus each municipality literally doesn't look beyond its own border, making the water more of a restrictive feature than a connecting one. 'The Drierivierenpunt is a unique place, and there is now a joint plan to further develop the area and connect locations with each other,' says Nicole op de Laak, head of Spatial Development Department of the municipality of Papendrecht and chair of the 'netwerk fysiek' management team for the Drechtsteden region. 'Now that we've reached that point, the trick is to take the next important steps.'

'The location on the junction of three rivers makes the Drechtsteden truly unique,' Nicole says. 'The area has many qualities: the presence of the water; the near proximity of cultural-historic heritage such as Kinderdijk and the historic centre of Dordrecht; the fact that it is situated next to the Biesbosch national park; the other centres with their own quality of life and housing; the maritime industry; and a good public transport system on the water. There are many options for enhancing the banks of the Drierivierenpunt for the purposes of living, working and recreation. This potential, however, is still untapped. There are several reasons for this. In many areas there is soil contamination, heavy industry and agreements with parties that have development rights. That often complicates the development of projects on the banks. But there are also excellent examples of something special arising. One example is the construction of a hotel-restaurant in a former water tower in Dordrecht. Named 'Villa Augustus', it is now a unique gem in the Drierivierenpunt. The Energiehuis, a cultural centre housed in a former power plant, and the movie theatre were added at a later stage. The development of these amenities has substantially enhanced the quality of time people spend on the banks.'

Atelier Drechtsteden's aim was to develop a joint vision and identify opportunities for the approach to the overall area. Participants were challenged to think about the area's future from a 'border-free' perspective (a perspective that ignores physical and intellectual borders). 'That worked,' Nicole says. 'Existing initiatives and ideas in the region were also identified, and we can build on these to achieve our vision: the so-called "visitekaartjes" ("calling cards")". As many as 80 have been itemised. So there's plenty of energy in this region.'

HAVE YOU BEEN ABLE TO TAKE THE NEXT STEPS?

'Not entirely,' Nicole says. 'I think this can be explained by several reasons. The results of the studio were linked to other visions and were presented to the board collectively. Processing that takes time. In order to get people to accept our recommendation of a "border-free" area,

there is a tendency, to split it up again. That's understandable, but there's a risk attached to that. If the challenge is split up too early, this will lead to a loss of coherence. It's important to take another step forward in refining an overarching vision aimed at all of the locations on the banks and agreeing on a cohesive programme. The profile of an individual location is primarily determined by the special qualities and environmental characteristics of that specific place. It is precisely by viewing these places in relation to one another that we can ensure a diverse range of activities on the water and the banks. Subsequently, each municipality can use the results to contribute to the larger whole.'

WHAT ARE THE CONDITIONS FOR PROGRESSING IN TERMS OF USING THE BANKS ALONG THE DRIERIVIERENPUNT?

'I think that placemaking and a bottom-up approach can help to make the places located on the banks more visible individually, or sometimes perhaps in relation to one another. You have to connect to the location's uniqueness to the greatest extent possible. That's the reason why people want to be there, live and recreate there. RiverArt is a good example. Art is being used to connect the banks between Rotterdam and the Drechtsteden with each other. Alternating places with special artworks give special meaning to individual places as well as the larger area.

What was the reason for establishing the Atelier Drechtsteden workshop?

Commissioned by the Drechtsteden, G.J. Jansen wrote a report in 2015 about the future of the 'Drecht' cities: 'Zichtbaar Samen Maritiem' ('Visible Together Maritime'). Jansen argued that there's a great deal of untapped potential in the Drechtsteden region and that it's lagging behind in terms of the quality of life and living, and failing to take advantage of economic opportunities. According to Jansen, municipalities and stakeholders should look at the area from a perspective that ignores the municipal borders and increases the visibility of the overall area. In order to implement this in practice, civil servants from the seven 'Drechtsteden' municipalities set up a studio in 2016 called the Atelier Drechtsteden. Supervised by studio manager Jeroen Laven from Stipo, they conducted research to assess opportunities for enhancing the socio-economic position of the Drechtsteden as a leading maritime region. The seven municipalities are Alblasserdam, Dordrecht, Hendrik-Ido- Ambacht, Papendrecht, Sliedrecht, Zwijndrecht and Hardinxveld-Giessendam, which will become part of the Drechtsteden region in the near future.

'We could improve the way we're linking up with existing initiatives as well: the 80 calling cards. Such as water bus stops: public spaces that can be made attractive to stay there a while. Or the location of the banks in Alblasserdam, which is an entry point for both Kinderdijk and the Drechtsteden.

'You can also attract temporary events, such as festivals, to places to give them added value. Or make the banks more accessible so that people will start walking and cycling there. Moreover, by enhancing the green spaces you can make the area more appealing. The Deltametropool Association is conducting a study on the landscape as a condition for settlement. Following the example of the Atelier Drechtsteden, the Drechtsteden region is one of the pilots of this study. There are also techniques for

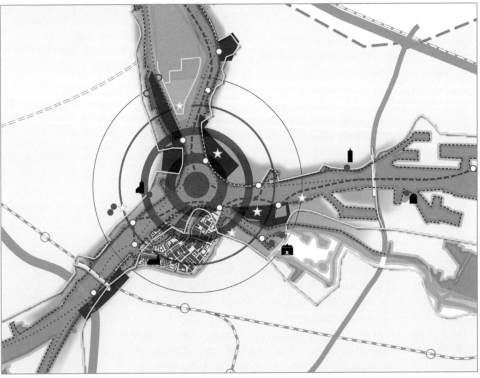

decontaminating the soil by creating green areas, which is a potential way of solving the soil contamination in locations along the banks. Finding momentum and co-financing from other parties are important conditions for the execution of the plans.'

'Once you agree on the main challenges,' Jantine Prins, strategic advisor of the municipality of Papendrecht says, 'then you can accomplish a great deal bottom-up. Indeed, the main challenge should actually be a test. To keep everyone on their toes you can make some kind of an agreement about quality assurance: "We were supposed to go for the best, not the quickest, weren't we?" You can also link up with the citymakers movement: people who have creative ideas about the area and strengthen the area or have the ability to make the area more visible. Now we need to look for a mixture of strategic and implementation capacities to really start making the next promising steps.'

DOS:

– Keep the overall picture in mind (integrated view) and do it together, including with non-governmental parties.
– Give people the freedom to do their work and don't lay down too many rules. Instil confidence in colleagues, market players and other external parties and don't call them to account for every step they take.
– Identify people's competencies: which people do you need? Bring in anyone involved at either the professional or grassroots level who shows persistence, also when developing plans.

DON'TS:

– Stay on your own island: that goes for both physical places and your professional domain.
– Fail to have a concrete follow-up plan. Involving parties is not noncommittal. They become enthusiastic and want to work together to ensure the plans succeed. You have to take their involvement seriously.

WORKING TOGETHER TO BUILD A GREAT CITY

Main shopping area in Tilburg

Tilburg's inner city is undergoing extensive demolition and construction work. The aim is to make the main shopping area 'compact and complete' in order to attract Tilburg residents and visitors to the city and to entice them to spend an enjoyable time there. The Tilburg municipality's team in charge of the main shopping area believes that a great deal has been achieved in partnership with project developers, shopkeepers and residents. The plan was completed within a year and its implementation is now progressing at full speed.

Tilburg's inner city street grid has traditionally consisted of east-west connections. The municipality wanted to change this structure. That's also in line with the strategy of making the main shopping area compact and complete. 'It's not only a matter of creating connections within the main shopping area, but also of connecting with the surrounding areas, such as the Spoorzone and the Dwaalgebied,' says Annemoon Dilweg, senior policy officer and spatial planning and project manager of the 21st-century inner city strategy. 'The Dwaalgebied has many culturally valuable buildings and a mix of residential housing, specialty shops and small-scale hospitality establishments. We're also planning a lively mix of shopping, culture and events for the main shopping area, as well as pleasant spots where visitors will want to linger. For instance, people who work in the city should have the opportunity to enjoy a nice lunch.'

The municipality is proceeding energetically and rigorously with the construction of the new cross connections. 'A new shopping street will be created in the city centre that connects the Pieter Vreedeplein with the Emmapassage and the Hendrikhof,' says Michiel van Hoof, inner city strategic account manager. Moreover, better connections are planned between shopping squares so that people can stroll criss-cross through the area. That will turn the squares into vibrant parts of the shopping area.' Michiel takes us to the rear of the Emmapassage, the covered shopping centre built about 25 years ago. The area doesn't look particularly enticing: boring streets, an unappealing square that's mainly surrounded by the backs of buildings. But Michiel primarily sees the potential and points to all the pedestrians: 'This has always been an important thoroughfare for pedestrians. The informal walking route used to go straight through the former V&D and Hema premises. Actually, we've just picked up on this desire path and are now turning it into an official and attractive route.'

The municipality has invested heavily in public spaces and the development of interconnections: a total of 18 million euros. For example, the municipality purchased two buildings on opposite sides of a busy shopping street in order to construct a cross street. It has already demolished one building and broken through the lower floors of the opposite premises. More green in an otherwise stony inner city will make the area not only more attractive but also important with a view to climate adaptation. 'The municipality can't do it alone,' says Tjalda Kalsbeek, real estate development project manager. 'Property investor Wereldhave in particular has been an important partner and will be investing in excess of 200 million euros in the area. Wereldhave owns shops on Emmapassage and Pieter Vreedeplein, the former V&D building and the Hema premises. 'Strangely, the pace of the entire plan accelerated when V&D collapsed,' says Laura Suijkerbuijk, urban development project assistant. 'The opportunity arose to invest in shops and housing. A total of some 350 housing units will be added to the main shopping area, concentrated in two tower blocks. Attracting new residents will help to improve public

From business district to mixed quarter

The municipality of Tilburg prepared an 'Economic-spatial development strategy for Tilburg's inner city in the 21st century'. The 21st-century inner city has merged the old city centre with the Spoorzone railway area (see the article 'Following in the footsteps of the Kind and Queen'). Tilburg is growing into a large, self-confident city with a strong centre. The strategy's starting point is to 'excite, engage, endure'. Tilburg is a university city and intends to use this potential for the benefit of the city's economy. But Tilburg also wants to be an exciting and surprising place for visitors. The strategy is built on four mutually reinforcing pillars: 1) Compact and complete: offering different functions and strengthening the quality of the main shopping area and the adjacent Dwaalgebied; 2) Development of talent and knowledge-based economy: strengthening the urban, knowledge-driven economy by further expanding, among others, the knowledge infrastructure in the Spoorzone; 3) Cultural and creative entrepreneurship: creativity and culture as the area's core values; and 4) Living environments for the next generation: offering different housing options for new target groups.

safety. Once more people start living in the area, it will also be livelier after closing time.'

'We really managed to seize the momentum together with Wereldhave,' Tjalda says. 'Retail was declining everywhere in the Netherlands. It was now or never. The first step in this rollercoaster ride was to attract Primark. The northern section of the new connecting road has already been built, though this was preceded by years of preparation.'

In addition to the partnership with Wereldhave, the private organisation tasked with Tilburg's inner city management, Binnenstad Management Tilburg (BMT), has also played an important role in the development of the area. 'We discuss the plans together and the BMT members gather ideas from their support base,' Tjalda says. 'The planning teams are also important. We benefit from previously gained experience with the development of the Piushaven harbour, where planning teams played a key role. The planning team for the main shopping area consists of entrepreneurs, developers, specialists and residents. They meet once every six weeks and have qualified advisory powers. They provide written advice to the municipality, but if the municipality doesn't adopt their advice, it has to argue its case quite convincingly.

For instance, the municipality had to decide whether the Northern arcade should be locked at night or not. The planning team felt it was important to keep the arcade open, and asked the municipality to include this option in the design. This means that the area might initially remain open in order to test the feasibility of this measure. Occasionally, members of the planning team may clash because of conflicting interests. Shopkeepers, for example, appreciate good visibility of their display windows, while landscape specialists want to create as much green space as possible. Discussing these subjects with each other creates mutual understanding.'

After some initial trepidation the new plans have gained a reasonable amount of support in the inner city. The majority of entrepreneurs and residents are enthusiastic, though some retailers remain critical of the plans. The construction of the residential tower blocks has also met with resistance, mainly from current residents who fear that the towers will obstruct their view. 'We're making every effort to inform people as thoroughly as possible,' Tjalda says. 'Tilburg's central message is: "Working together to build a great city". The municipalities and developers jointly promote this message.'

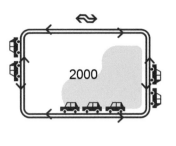

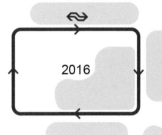

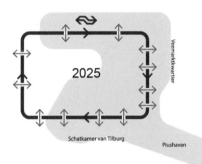

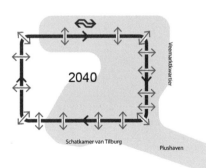

DOS:

– Collaborate with the planning teams responsible for the design of public spaces.
– Obtain information and listen to the various parties in the city. Explain what you're doing and why you're doing it. This will generate understanding among the people for the work being done.

DON'TS:

– The municipality shouldn't try to do everything alone. Ask other parties to become involved.
– Don't communicate per sub-project, but always try to focus on the larger picture in your external communications.

DOING IT TOGETHER SIMPLY RESULTS IN A BETTER PLAN

Placemaking embedded in new Groningen guide

After three decades, the municipality of Groningen was ready to review its policy for the design of public space. Urban planner Jaco Kalfsbeek and programme manager Gavin van Osnabrugge – who both work for the municipality of Groningen – explain how flexibility is the central tenet in the new design guide and in the city centre itself.

'A kind of military handbook, that's how people were inclined – rightly or wrongly – to use the old guide,' says city centre programme manager Gavin van Osnabrugge. This guide was the practical offshoot of the Space for Space masterplan in which the municipality of Groningen laid down its vision for public space in the city centre and which has been part of the comprehensive Better Inner City plan since 1993. In the past 25 years, this masterplan's approach has been applied to all issues related to the design of public space. But in recent years, support for it has dwindled. Many believed the framework was too rigid and provided insufficient latitude for customisation. 'The pressure on public space has increased,' Van Osnabrugge says, 'and today society is making different demands on the city centre as well. At the same time, urban development has to ensure that the cityscape remains cohesive, especially in light of the upcoming series of redevelopment projects. So the time had come for an evaluation and a review.'

In the framework of that process, the municipality invited STIPO to organise a three-day masterclass called 'Placemaking in Groningen' in the summer of 2016. It gave colleagues at the municipality an opportunity to gain experience in thinking about the city centre as a system, in analysing locations and in applying strategies to involve users (residents, entrepreneurs and visitors) in the development. The outcome of the masterclass was the foundation upon which the municipality of Groningen and LOLA Landscape Architects developed the new design guide for the city centre (see box).

'We are using a kind of Plan-Do-Check-Act sequence,' Van Osnabrugge explains. 'We have a project, apply the guide, develop a concrete design and from that point on we ask ourselves: okay, how is this going to work now? We're very aware that the city has benefitted a great deal from the Space for Space masterplan, but we want to manage public space in a more flexible way now. The new guide should outline the scope but also provide sufficient latitude to make diversity possible.'

Part of the guide is a kind of toolbox, and placemaking is one of the tools. 'It helps us to safeguard our approach for the future because the guide has a shelf life that exceeds the 4 to 5 years usually needed to plan a project. Another tool that we explicitly want to include in the guide is returning the sidewalk to the city, so that residents and users of buildings can use it to profile their identity – that which happens behind the façade.'

Last year, the municipality carried out a number of experiments in the city and used those experiences while developing the guide. The redevelopment of Astraat/Brugstraat, which began in September 2017, is one of these initial 'carefully considered experiments'. 'Every day, 25,000 cyclist and 10,000 pedestrians travel down that street,' Van Osnabrugge says. 'Sixty-one per cent of the visitors to the city centre of Groningen come by bike. That's partly the result of the fact that we have been indulging cyclists. But we're starting to reach the limit when it comes to parking facilities for bikes and effectively combining different kinds of traffic. Indeed, increasingly there are conflicts with pedestrians. So now we're saying: we want to prioritise the pedestrian. We had to get used to thinking from the notion of where we want to go and how we want to achieve something, instead of gearing our plans to an existing situation.'

New urban spaces

This design guide is expressly not a handbook that prescribes how and what should be designed. Rather, it's a guide containing basic choices. Inspiring examples and design principles ensure that one doesn't have to keep reinventing the wheel. The provided frameworks guarantee cohesion and recognisability in the city centre, but they also provide sufficient space for streets and neighbourhoods to create their own identity. The guide presents design principles, areas of concern and emphases for each type of street or square. The actual implementation can then start to take shape in partnership with local residents and other stakeholders.

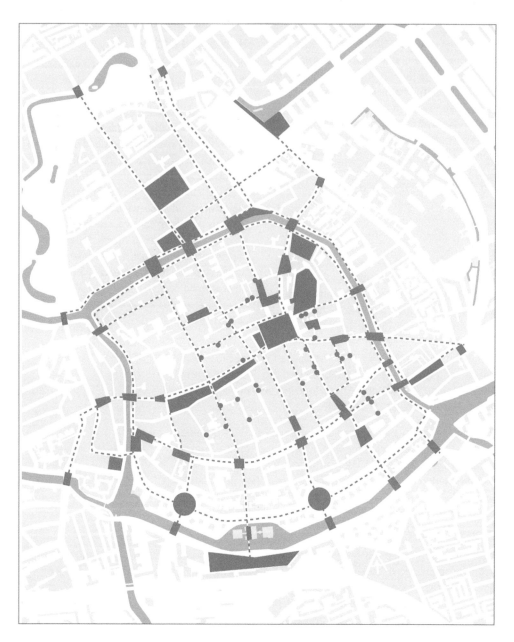

That inspired the idea to use the concept of shared space and alternative bike routes to give pedestrians more space. As a result, Astraat/Brugstraat were transformed into a paved ongoing route consisting of a sequence of places and street segments, where the bicycle path transitions to places that focus much more on visitors.'

'We know from previous experiments – in Folkingestraat, for example – that shared space works when alternated with

the flow of traffic,' Kalfsbeek says. 'When it's busy, the cyclist will wonder: "hey, where's my space?" And in this "confusion", he'll cycle very slowly, get off, or choose a different route. That's what we're looking for: we want to create a feeling that prompts people to make those kinds of decisions instead of placing a sign that bans cyclists in these kinds of streets on Saturdays, for example.

For the development of the new guide, it was important to first analyse how the city actually works. That produced a few standard measurements, such as a (hybrid) driving lane about 3.5 metres wide for emergency services, heavy goods traffic and cyclists, and an obstacle-free space for pedestrians about 2.5 metres wide. Together, these two determine whether there's any remaining space, and if so, how much space will be left over for the sidewalks. The emphasis is on freeing as much space as possible for pedestrians. The fact that the streets have not been asphalted and have no kerbs underscores once again the priority given to pedestrians.

'To find out how much latitude you have, you need to assay these kinds of things first. We drew a map in the guide which shows what we really need for the city to function and how much free space we subsequently have left. And regarding the latter, we said: it would be great to link that up with participation.'

'These are the places where we can apply placemaking in a highly specific way,' adds Van Osnabrugge. 'For example, on Minervaplein, where the art academy is located. During the placegame a "place team" was created there. It included entrepreneurs, residents and the location manager of the Minerva art academy.'

'We recently visited the director of Minerva,' Kalfsbeek says. 'Together we looked at how we can focus the long-term plans on what they want and what we want for the city centre. We decided that this place could become a real platform for the city. And by talking about it, you find yourself having completely different conversations as well. The Minerva building is extremely inwardly oriented. Now they're also going to start thinking about how they can connect their building and the public space better, for example by creating an attractive, open entrance to the restaurant in the front.'

'It's promising,' Van Osnabrugge agrees, 'to see that by thinking together about where you want to go as a city centre you also strike up other conversations at the level of individual property development about what's happening in the plinth.'

'Doing it together simply results in a better plan,' Kalfsbeek concludes. 'I also think that's what makes the "place teams" and involving target groups so special. In the past, we used to individually discuss plans with people, but now that we get everyone round the table together, we understand each other's needs better.'

KOEKAMP, LINKING THE CITY AND THE WOODS

Using the motto 'a new urban vibe', The Hague presented plans in 2015 for a new approach to outdoor space. Whereas the main tenets until then were 'clean, decent and safe', from that moment onwards the municipality wanted to also emphasise initiative and entrepreneurship, relaxation and opportunities for meeting up. Part of the new approach is a programme aimed at improving the city's entryways – the points that people use to enter the city. Koningin Julianaplein/Koekamp, directly opposite Central Station, is one of these.

'The idea behind the city entryways is as follows: visitors recognise the city as they enter and immediately feel at home,' says Irene Mulder, landscape architect and policy officer at the Urban Development & Planning Department of the municipality of The Hague. 'That requires top-quality outdoor space and an identity that is clearly identifiable with The Hague.' Anyone standing on Koningin Julianaplein near The Hague's Central Station, which is *the* city's reception area, is standing both on the threshold of the city and the threshold of one of the most beautiful urban woods in the Netherlands,' Mulder says. Koekamp is a key link between these two points.

Koekamp, Haagse Bos and Malieveld form a special entity by virtue of their unique location in the heart of the city, but also because of

their close connection to the city's early history. 'Koekamplaan is part of the "royal" axis that runs from the Noordeinde palace via Binnenhof, Lange and Korte Voorhout to the Huis ten Bosch palace and De Horsten country estate. These were the hunting grounds of the counts of Holland in the fourteenth century. There's still a forester walking around in 2017, in the middle of the city… Early on in the planning process we had Stichting In Arcadië, a research centre and planning bureau, conduct a culture-historical study. One interesting finding was that Koekamp is the oldest urban park in the Netherlands. The study has enhanced people's appreciation of the area's quality. It has also inspired the design of the green entryway,' Mulder says.

In her eyes, Koekamp is currently an uninviting place. The infrastructure, fences and bushes create physical and psychological barriers there. The aim is to transform it from a closed enclave in the city to a more public place that highlights its historical and ecological qualities.

Koekamp, Malieveld and Haagse Bos are the property of the forestry commission. The bombings, the construction of the Atlantic Wall and logging by the inhabitants meant that by the time the Second World War had ended, the woods had largely vanished. The forestry commission has made it a major wood again in recent decades. The municipality and the forestry commission have developed ideas for more drastic interventions on several occasions, such as creating an overpass spanning Utrechtsebaan, but until now only minor interventions have taken place.

About Koekamp

Koekamp is situated in front of Central Station in The Hague and borders Haagse Bos and Malieveld. The area was originally part of Haagse Bos and belonged to the hunting grounds of the counts of Holland. In the nineteenth century, landscape architect Jan David Zocher transformed Koekamp into an English landscape garden. Since 1976, a main thoroughfare, called Utrechtsebaan, has separated the park from Haagse Bos. The municipality and the forestry commission are developing a plan for a green entryway from Central Station into the city and the woods.

In 2015, Mulder witnessed a number of developments that increased the likelihood for a new approach to this area. In the framework of its plans for public space, the municipality held talks with various stakeholders in the city, including the forestry commission. The renovation of Central Station also altered the vision on public space in the station's surroundings, and financial resources became available after the programme for the city entryways was determined.

During this time, the forestry commission was also reinventing its role in society. 'Protect, experience and use' became the commission's new motto. 'By engaging in a dialogue with the forestry commission and taking advantage of the momentum, the pieces of the puzzle started to fall into place, and now a plan has been developed for 'The green entryway' into The Hague. Together, our intention is to make this a top spot,' Mulder explains.

Mulder also ensured that this project was included in the municipality's regional policy on green space. The 'Duin, Horst en Weide' ('Dune, Hurst and Pasture') landscape register was established in 2014 for the area between The Hague and Leiden, the aim of which is to develop its nature and landscape. One of the underlying objectives is to improve the relation between the city and its surroundings. Haagse Bos and Koekamp are the entryway to this landscape from The Hague. That's why resources were included in the landscape register's implementation programme for the green entryway's plan. In the meantime, the Hollandse Duinen National Park is a reality now as well. The partners working together in this area, which extends from Hoek van Holland to Hillegom, welcomed the ambitious plans for the park in June 2017. Koekamp will become a key entryway into this national park.

In the design, created by landscape architect Steven Delva in cooperation with Ingenieursbureau Den Haag, Koekamp is also being 'pieced in' so that it creates a link with the city centre. This will create more cohesion with the station square, the design of which is emphatically green. The result resembles a 'green carpet', as opposed to the 'red carpet' that runs from Turfmarkt and Anna van Buerenplein to the train station.

The park is surrounded by many ministries and other government offices. The park is going to be redesigned in the style of Zocher – undulating lines, ponds, bridges and bushes – so that it becomes a more appealing place to walk around, to have lunch or to work on your laptop for an hour or so. Cafés and restaurants, as well as an information centre, are going to open at the location where the forestry commission now has its offices and a workshop. There are plans for a pavilion and a small harbour elsewhere in the park. A pleasant route will be built from Central Station to the wood.

A major task is going to be streamlining the busy flows of traffic in the vicinity of Koekamp. The tunnels there have already reduced the number of cars driving by the park, but during rush hour, pedestrians, cyclists and trams tend to get into each other's way. Another major obstacle is Utrechtsebaan, which separates the park from Haagse Bos. The ideal solution would be to lower the

road, so that the historical connection would be reinstated, but that's a costly and technically complicated solution. It was decided that a wider overpass with more green will be built over the Utrechtsebaan level with the Malietoren.

Placemaking is not only a physical but also a social process. Indeed, the municipality has involved local residents, entrepreneurs and other stakeholders in the planning process through a series of workshops. Stakeholders have been invited to take walks through the park so that together the best route for the paths can be determined.

Koekamp is also part of the Central Innovation District that's situated between the three most important NS stations in The Hague: CS, HS and Laan van NOI. Mulder hopes that the ultra-urban development planned here will create more opportunities in the future to reduce car-related infrastructure, to bridge the Utrechtsebaan and to reinstate the connection between Koekamp and Haagse Bos.

DO:

– Immerse yourself in the meaning and identity of an area by conducting culture-historical research on it. Involve parties that feel connected to the area when formulating the task.

DON'T:

– Don't build an infrastructure that will negatively impact public space, and which can only be rectified later through expensive and complicated interventions.

THE HAGUE CREATES EXCITING PLACES FOR CHILDREN

How do you design a child-friendly city? Now that expansion is increasingly making way for infill development, and the available space is becoming scarcer by the day, demand is also becoming more pressing. The Hague is emphatically trying to make its public space more child friendly. We paid a visit to Ruud Ridderhof, programme manager of public space at the Department of City Management, and Bastiaan de Jong, neighbourhood manager in Mariahoeve.

'I think it's really dreadful to narrow down child friendliness to safe playgrounds,' Ridderhof begins. 'For me, playing is an extremely serious form of research. So create environments that are worth studying. Safety is necessary, no doubt about that, but combine that with excitement. And don't focus solely on children, focus on the whole person.'

'But do make sure that you view the city through the lens of your children, and not from an adult perspective,' De Jong responds. He cites two examples that illustrate how the perspective of children and adults differ. 'We thought that we had built a safe playground, but the children saw a nearby bike path where road bikers were cycling by as a serious impediment. And they pointed out that the barriers at a tram crossing were easy to by-pass.'

As neighbourhood manager he often invites children, through schools and clubs, usually in the age range of 11 or 12, to examine places together. What needs to happen there to make it more fun and exciting? In these cases too, a child often sees things that an adult doesn't. 'A child might perceive a dark corner that we view as unsafe to be a great place to play.'

What happens once children have expressed their opinion? 'Sometimes it takes some pushing and cajoling to get the administrative organisation to get something done in that respect,' De Jong says. 'It takes a change of mindset to achieve that. It's a lengthy process and hasn't been completely resolved yet in The Hague. What helps in that respect is that we include specialists from the trade, such as city park managers and policy officers, in these kinds of processes. That helps them to become more conscious of how children view things.'

Ridderhof flags another problem: children's limited attention span. 'There are many fun ways of involving them in the design of a place, for example by letting them design on the computer with the aid of digital building blocks, but the problem is the time period between the design and the implementation. That's often too long for them. By then, they've lost their attention and commitment. To be honest, I'm not sure how to solve that problem.'

'Indeed, you can't wait six months after a design session to make a plan and then only implement it a year later,' De Jong says. 'What we're doing is organising what you might call mini-classes with children and administrators of public space. The administrators explain to the children what the big people rules are and how they should take that into consideration in their design. That results in better plans and a better chance of them being carried out.'

Ridderhof agrees that much has improved in The Hague. There are less 'shameful green' areas nowadays, green areas that were plunked down somewhere due to a lack of imagination. He praises the natural playground called Zuiderpret in Zuiderpark, where an artificial stream was built and where children can play with water, sand, mud and tree branches. In his opinion, a good example is the initiative by Museum Beelden aan Zee, which has a large outdoor patio with fairy-tale sculptures by sculptor Tom Otterness which children are free to climb on. 'That's tangible art – it's inviting and it's something that thrills families and children.'

According to Ridderhof, one of the challenges with infill development is not only to create places but also routes. 'Routes are more exciting than places. It means paths, corridors and casual routes. That's a tricky issue with infill development, because the latter often means using up all of the available space and cutting off the connections. In the past 20 years, we've managed to return a great deal of space to cyclists, so I think now the time has come to do the same for pedestrians. This is also something you have to keep in mind for senior citizens, for example in the vicinity of care homes.'

'By the way, do you have children involved in Ruimte voor de Stad ('Space for the City, an agenda for the spatial development of The Hague, ed.)?' De Jong asks.

'Not as far as I know,' Ridderhof responds. 'But that's difficult with these kinds of abstract subjects. It's not realistic to have them engage in a discussion at this level.'

'I don't agree with you on that,' De Jong says. 'As long as you take their level into consideration. For example, don't talk about spatial structures, but about building new houses.'

City of piece and justice

The Hague is the residence of the Netherlands: the king has his palace there and the government and parliament are seated there. The city has a strong international orientation and has the reputation as a city of peace and justice. The Peace Palace, which houses the International Court of Justice and the Permanent Court of Arbitration, is located in the city, for example. The Hague has more than 500,000 inhabitants, which makes it the third-largest city in the Netherlands, after Amsterdam and Rotterdam. The population is relatively young. Almost half of the city's people have an immigrant background. Although The Hague is part of the Randstad conurbation, it's the only Dutch city on the North Sea. There's plenty of green and nature for a large city: it has beaches and dunes, but also parks and country estates.

'I think that on this point the Environmental Planning Bill will benefit development,' Ridderhof elaborates. 'It forces you to take a more integrated approach and work together more intelligently. That's exactly what you need with increased density. It also gets public servants out of their cubicles.'

'Make the citizen, and therefore also the child, much more of a source of inspiration for public space,' De Jong concludes.

DO:

– Ask the children, not the school principals or public servants, what will make a place look best. Involve them as early in the process as possible. Make it clear exactly what is happening and when.

DON'T:

– Don't isolate the assignment, so don't only look at what the children need from a place. Ensure that the process isn't overdrawn. Don't think you're there just because you've installed a colourful fence.

MAASTRICHT: PLACEMAKING IS A LENGTHY PROCESS

'Life in Maastricht largely takes place outdoors. This is particularly evident in the traditional celebration of carnival,' says Jake Wiersma, urban planner at the municipality of Maastricht where one of his main concerns is the quality of public space.

Placemaking is a new term for something that has occupied a central position in Maastricht's urban development policy for years. Traffic structure is a crucial element because in placemaking everything revolves around places and flows. There are now great opportunities for putting this policy into practice, since Maastricht's infrastructure is undergoing a thorough revision. Around the year 2000, the motorway running along the Maas River was tunnelled to make room for a boulevard, in order to revive the relationship between city and river. The A2 motorway was recently tunnelled as well, which freed up a sizeable strip of land above ground. By moving the Noorderbrug trajectory slightly northwards, the inner city is once again connected to its surroundings. This has also created a substantial low-traffic area, which is an important precondition in placemaking.

All of this dovetails with Maastricht's plan to create better public spaces. Maastricht is the second-most visited city in

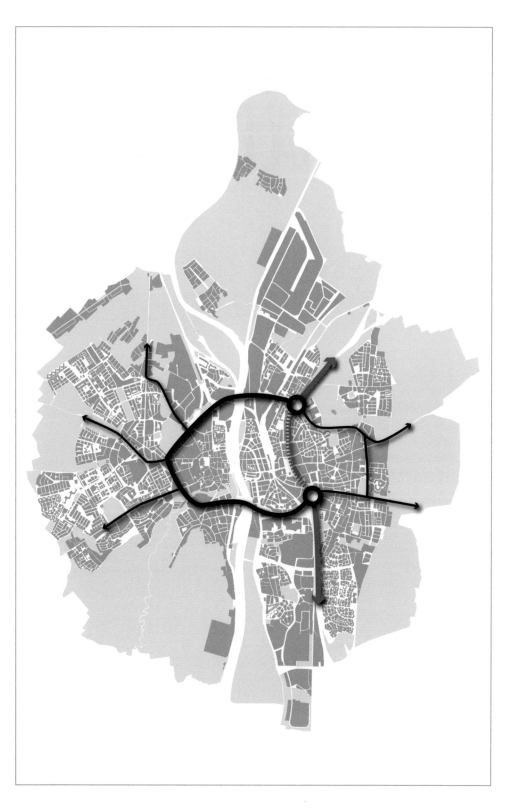

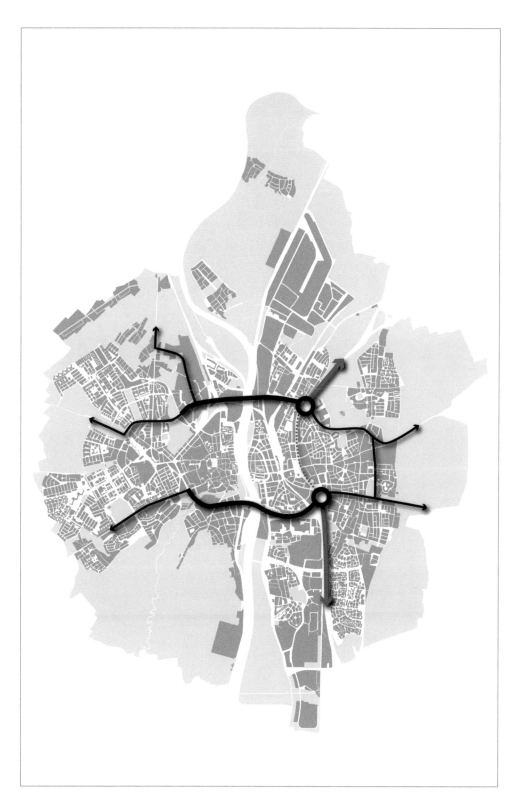

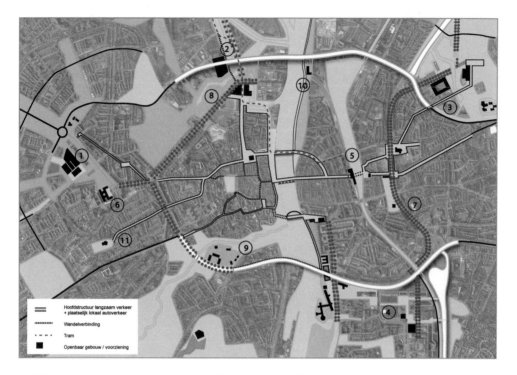

Hoofdstructuur langzaam verkeer
+ plaatselijk lokaal autoverkeer

Wandelverbinding

Tram

Openbaar gebouw / voorziening

the Netherlands, after Amsterdam, and just like the capital the municipality of Maastricht wants to prevent its historical centre from becoming totally congested. New forms of placemaking, also extending beyond today's city centre, will have to help achieve this objective.

Placemaking requires more than just the banning of cars. You also have to take slow traffic flows into consideration, according to Wiersma, which are essential for creating favourable conditions for hospitality outlets and amenities. These are a prerequisite for developing lively and attractive public spaces.

With respect to the latter, extensive experience has been gained with Plein 1992 in the new city district Céramique to the east of the Maas River. Here, the new library/ city hall constitutes an important source of vibrant life. A new footbridge across the Maas River facilitates the flow of pedestrian traffic, which is positive for the hospitality industry, but not always appreciated by local residents.

The most drastic and eye-catching project has been the tunnelling of the A2 motorway, whose construction started in 2000. The recent opening of the King Willem-Alexander Tunnel freed up a substantial strip of public space that will be put to excellent use in the coming decades. 'That's quite a challenge,' admits Wiersma.

A 'Green Carpet' has been planned: a broad, tree-lined avenue surrounded by buildings, with a lot of green and a generous path for cyclists and pedestrians. The buildings will consist of stately homes to create a residential lane with allure. The area will have limited traffic rather than being traffic free. That's not really necessary. With a density of 15,000 motor vehicles a day, it's essential to install pedestrian signs, traffic lights and zebra crossings, but if the numbers are lower it should be possible to cross safely without these devices. By keeping traffic intensity beneath this 'tipping point' the municipality wants to create an entirely different perception and use of the street. All these points will be laid down in a design vision statement prepared by the developer and the municipal council.

The area between the back of the railway station and the current shopping centre on the A2 motorway will have a more mixed and vibrant character. The choice to locate the central facilities here was deliberate. A walkway has been proposed, to be built either above or beneath the railway tracks, which would improve the connection with the inner city. This, too, will create the necessary precondition for placemaking.

By moving the Noorderbrug trajectory, Maastricht will gain more public space to the north of the centre. The old fortification area will be linked more directly with the inner city and space will be created for a park that could serve as a venue for events.

All of these projects will provide more room for new municipal facilities outside the historical city centre. For instance, the public library and the Bonnefanten Museum will be relocated to the Céramique district. But you can't go on shuffling facilities around forever, Wiersma warns. 'Removing shops from the inner city is usually not a good idea. A city has to cherish what it already has and expand where possible.'

The aim of expansion should be to create a new urbanity outside the city centre, for example by providing space for start-up entrepreneurs. 'The southern part of the province of Limburg,' Wiersma says, 'has to convey an urban feeling without the need to live in the busy inner city: relaxed green

Infrastructural changes

Maastricht is undergoing major infrastructural changes. The A2 motorway has been rerouted through a tunnel, for example. Since late 2016, high-speed traffic in the east of the city has been flowing through a stacked, two-tier tunnel instead of across residential areas. This intervention has freed up a strip of land 2.3 kilometres long. Moreover, the Noorderbrug trajectory, which is an east-west connection to Belgium, has been moved slightly northwards in order to give the inner city more space and ease traffic congestion. All this dovetails with Maastricht's plans to keep cars out of the city, create better public spaces, and enhance the city's relationship with the river and water in general. Placemaking has been playing an important role in this process.

living with the inner city just around the corner. The districts around the inner city in particular have to offer better connections to the historical centre.'

A new aspect is that residents and entrepreneurs have to receive more leeway to develop their own initiatives and gain ownership of public space. One condition, however, is that the initiatives must have the support of the entire street and not only the entrepreneur, explains Wiersma. For example, if businesses want to expand their sidewalk terraces they have to ensure that they coordinate their plans and that sufficient space remains for pedestrians. This way the street arrives collectively at a solution.

'It's a challenge for the municipality to safeguard the balance between public and private and to avoid putting pressure on the public quality of the city,' concludes Wiersma. 'We accomplish this by working more closely with entrepreneurs, residents and other parties involved, and by presenting different scenarios with different perspectives. By getting together more frequently we can work on a common goal.'

DO:

– When embarking on a placemaking project, instead of only looking at the place itself, also look at the conditions for making it a success. Important aspects to consider are the inclusion of slow traffic routes and the proximity of existing facilities.

DON'T:

– Don't try to create places everywhere. Encourage the development of one or more places in districts where facilities are disappearing, but restrict their number: it's quite all right if some places are in more sheltered areas. Don't deny your identity. Maastricht has a chic quality, so sometimes bold initiatives are better suited for Heerlen.

INNER CITY PLAN OF ATTACK

How Doetinchem is giving the inner city back to residents and entrepreneurs

These days, people lie resting in their beach chairs along the Oude IJssel in Doetinchem with their feet in the sand and a drink in their hand. It's one of the new places in the inner city of Doetinchem, and owes its existence to the 'Inner City Plan of Attack'. The municipality works closely with residents and entrepreneurs in the inner city on this plan. The point of departure is no small individual projects, but a long-term process of cooperation between authorities, residents, entrepreneurs and other parties. The ultimate aim is to give back the inner city to residents and entrepreneurs.

Doetinchem has a clear ambition: become the hospitality capital of the Achterhoek region. 'Doetinchem already has the amenities,' says councillor Peter Drenth. 'We serve the entire Achterhoek, about 200,000 people. But they only come to the inner city when there's something to experience, when the inner city is more than just an accumulation of shops. It's also about emotion and perception.'

The aim is for the inner city to become a hospitable and dynamic place. Another priority is to strengthen perceptions of the Achterhoek in the inner city and connect the Oude IJssel to the city centre. Different parties are working on this aim in a variety of ways. Examples include better marketing, finding solutions

for cycling in the inner city, organising events, making the city greener and setting up a food hall for entrepreneurs in the former V&D building. 'Together with residents and entrepreneurs, we're creating all kinds of incentives,' explains Bart Teunissen, project manager for the inner city. 'We're investing heavily in the core shopping area, but also on the edges of the inner city. These two things go hand in hand.'

A nice example is the approach to Terborgseweg, an important approach road to the centre. An agreement was reached with residents and entrepreneurs to make this a green avenue. 'On the side of the road where there are a lot of retail businesses, we're going to substantially widen the sidewalks, creating an attractive approach route from the station to the inner city,' Drenth says. 'We're therefore also creating space for shopkeepers. The baker can put some tables and chairs in front of the store where customers can sit comfortably.'

'During the municipal elections in 2014, the plans for the inner city started to accelerate,' Drenth says. 'During an election debate we said that we needed an Inner City Plan of Attack to improve the inner city. The point of departure was to retain the good things that we already have and improve the things of lesser quality. The shopping area called De Veentjes was one of these places. This outdated shopping area is situated just outside the centre. In recent years, an increasing number of shops were forced to shut down, causing vacancy to rise dramatically. What remained were a few snack bars and a stray shop. In light of the aim to make the inner city more compact, residents, entrepreneurs, building owners and public servants are now working together to transform this shopping area into a residential area. In recent months, the municipality organised several work meetings with everyone involved in the area. Within three months they came up with a detailed plan that will make it possible for people to live in the plinth and which will redesign the outside space.

'Our strength is that we are constantly improving the way we handle temporary transition situations,' Teunissen says. 'As a result, these aren't small, individual projects. But they dovetail with the broader development of the centre, which we are experiencing together with the city's residents and entrepreneurs. Mixed teams of residents, entrepreneurs, building owners and public servants are working throughout the city on making it resilient for the future.'

'We all agreed that we shouldn't develop the plan for the improvement of the inner city at the university or at city hall,' says professor by special appointment Gert-Jan Hospers from Radboud University.

'Instead, we devised the plan with people in the inner city while walking through it. We asked residents and visitors to show us a place that they're extremely proud of and a place they thought could be improved. As we walked through the streets, people shared their vision of the inner city.' Based on this input, Gert-Jan Hospers and two of his colleagues wrote the 'Doetinchem at Eye Level' strategy, which is the foundation for the long-term process of cooperation with residents, entrepreneurs and other partners in the inner city.

This new approach also fits in with the municipality's new role. 'The municipality is no longer the key player in the city, but one of many players,' Drenth says. 'The municipal council fully supports this approach. Even before decisions had been made about what direction to take, the council pledged a structural amount of 1 million euros a year to invest in the inner city. 'On condition that the partners in the city co-financed the plan,' he says. 'As the municipality, we will contribute up to half of the amount. The other half has to come from the city.'

A wish often expressed by inhabitants is to involve the Oude IJssel more with the inner city. This already began to crystallise when three young couples took the initiative to develop a new spot along the river, where people can stay and have a drink and a bite. 'In

light of the Inner City Plan of Attack it made absolute sense to offer space to this initiative,' Drenth says. 'Old garage sheds of the police are being used: their rolling doors can be opened and a kitchen has been installed in one of them. Outside, there are beach chairs and umbrellas, and the local ice cream vendor set up a tent there. It's a simple and extremely popular place that people love to visit.'

'That's also because it's a place where people can combine relaxation with amenities for eating and drinking,' Teunissen adds. 'People go there on Sunday morning to do yoga and drink a cup of coffee. They play football there and take their children along. People can take off their shoes and sit by the water. Everyone has embraced this place.' In the spring of 2016 the municipality built a strolling jetty where people can sit and enjoy the water when the weather's nice. There are plans to build footpaths around the Oude IJssel, as well as a footbridge over the river, and people have expressed the wish for more recreational options along the water and a quay where they can sit.

The first three years of the Inner City Plan of Attack are history now, but the end is nowhere in sight. The basis of a long-term partnership between the authorities and residents and entrepreneurs has yielded many excellent projects, initiatives and new energy. Compared to a few years ago, entrepreneurs have a completely different attitude about everything that's happening in the inner city. 'Entrepreneurs are now bearing part of the risk in developments,'

Drenth says. 'We've also noticed that public servants are approaching their work differently. They're now contributing their expertise and skills to the discussion instead of just making sure that initiatives comply with procedures and rules. They're also engaging with residents and entrepreneurs in a much different way, because they're members of the mixed teams. This joint approach increases support, which ultimately accelerates plans.'

DOS

- Honour agreements and remain open to ideas.
- Be clear in advance (about frameworks, money, time, the chances of failure).
- Stay focused on the task: determine during each phase who will be part of a mixed team.
- Harvest low-hanging fruit, be visible, highlight changes and make people enthusiastic.
- Work from small to large in order to achieve consensus.

DON'TS:

- Don't plan any unnecessary meetings: the free time of residents and entrepreneurs is a scarce commodity. So only plan meetings when they're necessary.
- Don't allow setbacks to disillusion you and keep the larger aim in mind.
- Don't make promises you can't keep.

AREA
DEVELOPMENT

AN URBAN LIVING ROOM SIX MINUTES FROM SCHIPHOL AIRPORT

We're meeting three civil servants at the World Trade Center, where Zuidas Amsterdam has its own accommodations. This is no coincidence, because in placemaking you have to be in the place where it all happens, according to Eline Hoogendijk, Zuidas programme manager. Also joining us is chief urban designer Paco Bunnik, who supervises large building projects in Zuidas, and plinth manager Saskia Rill, who works on increasing the area's liveliness by filling the commercial spaces located in the plinths of the buildings.

How do you turn an area initially perceived as a bleak stone desert into a vibrant, multipurpose urban neighbourhood? 'By developing a joint strategy in which everyone becomes a partner,' Rill kicks off the discussion. 'It started in 2010 with the 15by15 programme, in which we defined 15 goals to be achieved by 2015,' Hoogendijk explains. 'Some of them concerned the area's vibrancy. In those days you couldn't even buy a sandwich here. We civil servants were also bothered by this lack of amenities.'

The position of plinth manager was invented in those days, the first of its kind in the Netherlands. The reason was the high vacancy rate of the street-level plinths, which gave the area a desolate air, even though the market showed an interest in these premises. Many retailers contacted the municipality because they were interested in a plinth. 'That seems strange,' Rill says, 'because the municipality doesn't own the properties, but frequently the entrepreneurs had no other way of finding out what exactly was available for rent.'

'That's because the property owners and real estate agents did not actively promote the plinths," Bunnik says, 'but rather concentrated on filling the offices on the upper floors. They considered the plinths less interesting from a commercial point of view. On the other hand, the plinths are extremely important to us; they infuse the area with life and energy.'

'Many of the empty premises didn't even display a "for rent" sign,' Rill recalls. 'I was tempted to grab a pen and paper and write "for rent" on them. That's why I decided to make a plinth map: an overview of the premises available for rent, their prices, the number of square metres, and the name of the contact person to be approached.'

In recent years, thanks partly to Rill's work, the property owners have addressed the plinth issue more actively. The municipality tries to guide the allocation of the plinths as much as possible. 'In those days,' Hoogendijk says, 'we thought we had to attract flagship stores. Our reasoning was that once Louis Vuitton descends on Zuidas, everything else will fall into place. But Zuidas is a *high-traffic* location without *high traffic*. Apparently, men prefer buying a suit on PC Hooftstraat accompanied by their partner.' 'Dont forget,' Rill says, 'that we are located between Beethovenstraat and Gelderlandplein, and that's stiff competition for us.'

According to Bunnik, the current search concentrates on 'shops and facilities with great drawing power and a human touch'. Their level has to match the environment. For example, bicycle shops, convenience stores or cheese shops.

How do I get the right shop in the right place? Rill pursued the developers and owners persistently, 'like a Jehovah's Witness', questioning them about their plans. And she

From business district to mixed quarter

Zuidas (literally the southern axis) is a business district plus residential housing along the A10 South Ring Road in Amsterdam. It was once the largest of six key government projects. The Zuidas covers an area of 268 hectares and is home to the World Trade Center and the headquarters of ABN Amro and AkzoNobel, among others. Developments are still in full swing in this area. Initially, mainly offices were built here, but in recent years a large number of residential housing units have been added. The most important upcoming intervention is the underground relocation of a section of the A10. Moreover, the Amsterdam Zuid Railway Station will be expanded into a high-quality public transport terminal. The Zuidas project should be fully completed by about 2035. The overall direction of this area is in the hands of the Municipality of Amsterdam's Zuidas department, formerly Dienst Zuidas. The Hello Zuidas Foundation, a collaborative effort of the municipality, businesses, residents and other Zuidas users, is primarily focused on area management. To improve the area's vibrancy and quality of living, the municipality has initiated the Leef Zuidas programme.

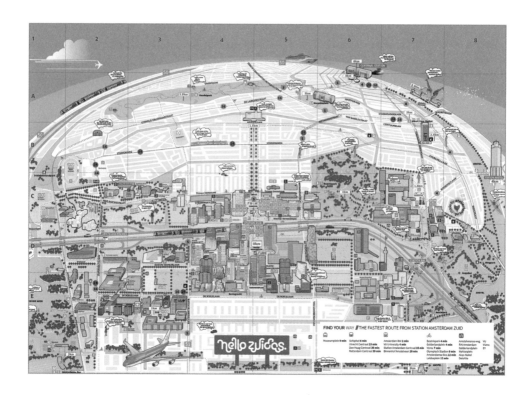

actively started to look for suitable shops, which she subsequently matched up with owners. Much of this work is informal and takes place behind the scenes. It consists primarily of talking and liaising with people. Leasehold agreements concluded after a tender has been won now include a clause known as the 'Saskia Rill provision', which entails that the municipality has to be involved in the future allocation of the plinth if the stipulations laid down in the tender are not met by the occupant.

The main obstacle in filling a plinth vacancy is not the price, as is often assumed. The price is frequently lower than expected. 'That's Zuidas' best kept secret,' Rill laughs. It's actually the size of the plinths that's usually the problem. 'They're frequently too large for one user,' Bunnik explains. 'You have to split them up. For instance, this could mean creating six front doors in a sixty-metre plinth. That makes everything more small-scale.' Dealing with foreign owners is often more difficult than with Dutch ones. 'A German owner doesn't want an Amsterdam pioneer in the plinth but an established party that signs up for five years,' Rill says.

Zuidas Amsterdam encourages and embraces initiatives that contribute to a positive perception of the area. For example, a small field in the shade of the Symphony residential tower block was sown with maize, which pigs are allowed to devour on World Animal Day. A circus, a fair and an Oktoberfest have also installed themselves in

Zuidas. The 'waaigat', or windy hole, as the Zuidas is jokingly referred to, is gradually changing into a mixed quarter where urban planners and placemakers from far and wide come to gain inspiration.

And rightfully so, says Bunnik. 'It's unique to find such an urban living room only six minutes from Schiphol Airport. Nowadays, the area is bustling at lunchtime. That's because we're giving increasing priority to pedestrians and cyclists. We extended the pedestrian zone all the way to the area's perimeter; we are broadening the pavements, and we're reducing car traffic. Mahlerlaan, for example, will become a one-way street to create more space for outdoor cafés and green areas.'

Zuidas Amsterdam is making every effort to increase its quality of living. A case in point are the transformer houses that obscure the view. We're currently discussing with the owners about the possibility of hiding them, although this isn't easy for safety reasons.

Asked whether placemaking in Zuidas is a municipal or a joint matter, Bunnik replies that it will still take a bit of 'pushing and pulling' to achieve the latter. 'A critical mass is needed. We've just reached the turning point.' 'A large number of housing units will be delivered in the autumn of this year,' Hoogendijk says, 'which could very well be the extra push we need.' 'We have had inquiries from a library, museums and cinemas,' Bunnik says. Developers are increasingly willing to contribute ideas at the front-end.

Rill has observed that increasingly Zuidas is becoming a
normal part of Amsterdam, with complaints about noise
pollution and so forth. She has a clear vision of how the area
will look in five years' time: 'Residents are playing a game
of boules on Gershwinplein, a lovely sunny square with a
Mediterranean flair with an art market and well-stocked plinths.
My position will then have become obsolete because by then
everyone will be aware of the important role of the plinths.'

DO:

– Ensure that you have good contact with all stakeholders.
  Government should invest heavily in the quality of public
  spaces.

DON'T:

– The government shouldn't try to manage everything. Remote
  working, away from the area in question, is not desirable.

SPOORZONE DELFT, A NEW SPACE IN A HISTORIC CITY CENTRE

Until 2015, a railway line cut straight through the old part of Delft, allowing train passengers to peek into the buildings along the railway. Anyone traveling to Delft today, though, plunges underground. A new 'railway' zone – Spoorzone – has emerged above ground as a result, right in the middle of the old centre of Delft. 'It's always interesting, no matter where you are in the world, when an open space is created in an old historic city for you to develop,' says Gido Ten Dolle, director of urban development for the municipality of Delft. 'How are you going to connect other areas to the new area and make sure it becomes just as vibrant?'

About Delft's Spoorzone

Delft's Spoorzone covers an area 24 hectares large. The clients of this project are the Ministry of Infrastructure and the Environment and the municipality of Delft. The project management of the railway tunnel and the public transport hub is in the hands of ProRail and the municipality of Delft/Spoorzone Delft Development Company. The Ministry of Infrastructure and the Environment, the municipality of Delft, the province of South Holland, Stadsgewest Haaglanden and the urban region of Rotterdam are all co-financing the project.

WHAT WERE THE ORIGINAL PLANS FOR SPOORZONE?

'We set our targets 12 years ago. Initially, the main focus was on building an underground railway line. Put simply, the project basically entailed breaking open the ground, throwing in some tubes and closing it up again. We were only able to start our work above ground recently. Finally we were able to start implementing the masterplan from 2015, with its new station, dwellings, offices, green areas and water.

'While working on the project, we were suddenly hit by the economic crisis. We had to make huge sacrifices during the crisis years in terms of our initial plans and ambitions. Now the tunnel is there and the economic situation has improved. There's room for investment again. And that's what led to the 'Delft Herstelt' advisory group's recommendation led by Wim Deetman in 2016. The goals have been revised. Now we're really going to get moving on the area above ground.'

COULD YOU TELL US SOME MORE ABOUT HOW THE ORIGINAL PLANS WERE REVISED?

'We're currently reassessing the Integral Development Plan. This reassessment is a key item on the agenda. A great deal has changed in many areas over the past 12 years, such as sustainability, mobility and parking. In September 2016, the development firm Ontwikkelingsbedrijf Spoorzone Delft BV advised us to ride the momentum, instead of hurrying to put plots on the market. You also have to see whether the 2014 programme still makes sense. Do the housing development projects still tie in with the needs? Can we really make this an area for the inhabitants of Delft, for example by providing

housing for the elderly as well? In November and December, we had sessions with the advisory board for Spoorzone, experts and the executive board of the municipality. In July 2017, the revised plan was drafted by the executive board.'

ARE YOU ALSO LOOKING AT HOW TO CONNECT THE AREA TO THE REST OF THE CITY?

'We're looking explicitly at how the new area can be connected to other parts of the city. Spoorzone is expanding the centre, but it's also establishing a connection between the old centre and city districts that used to be split off from the centre by the railway. The emergence of a new area in the middle of the city has certainly prompted people to start thinking. For example, a care centre that's now situated on the outskirts of the city would like to move to a more central location because its elderly residents want a livelier environment. Or imagine a housing corporation that plans to build new rental properties across from rental properties built in the 1980s. The gap in quality between these properties would be visibly huge. Try explaining that to your residents.'

DO THE INHABITANTS OF DELFT FEEL INVOLVED IN THIS AREA?

'The inhabitants are feeling increasingly involved, and that's an organic process. You can compare it to dismantling a house. First you strip it and take everything out, at which point it hardly feels like a house anymore. Then you create a shell out of it. And finally you start to make it your own again by choosing wallpaper and laying carpets. That psychological moment literally came about when we started to lay bricks and plant trees. In the autumn, there was non-stop buzz about the area on social media. Until then, people had only seen the drawings of the bricks and the trees. Then they saw it all for real: so that's the kind of brick they used, that's how they laid the bricks and this is what the trees look like. People started actually thinking about it. "Was that the right tree to use?" Psychologically speaking, the area becomes more a part of you. Just like when you lay a carpet and choose a décor for your kitchen. Now we're involving people in the design of the park. I think that we'll see more residents getting involved in the coming year.

'I hope that we can hang on to the positive feeling that exists right now. That could be tricky. It will take five to seven more years before most of this area has been developed. It will be another three or four years before we even start building in some places. It will be interesting to see whether people's patience will wear thin or not. How long will the residents keep it up? Now some places are being completed and they look good. But soon the trucks will be back again with sand and building piles. People may start to wonder whether this will ever end.

LAST QUESTION: WHAT ARE THE LESSONS LEARNED?

'Looking back, we definitely should have split up the development of this area into sub-areas and handled the development and financing of the whole area in phases. But that wasn't possible because we had to come to an agreement with the state in one single deal. That forced us to take an all-or-nothing approach, with all of the major risks that this entailed. We also decided to be pragmatic and put the development of the area into a limited company. That enabled us to tighten the reins and determine the pace of developments. It also allowed us to stay more independent and keep developments at more of an arm's length from political decision-making. It was a good choice, but it certainly had a downside as well. It has made it more difficult for the inhabitants of the city to become co-owners of the area that we're developing. That's something we're going to have to pay close attention to in the coming years. The people of Delft are going to want have more and more of a say in the urban planning, and they will get it too. I see that as a positive development. We're going to literally give the Spoorzone back to the city.

'The project continues to be a massive learning curve. The area is in a constant state of flux. It's consistently dynamic.

Once we've laid the paving stones, for example, the next task is already waiting. That's a huge challenge for the authorities too. Authorities are well-trained at carrying out projects: when something is finished, there's no need to look back. But now we need to train the people to understand that it will never be finished. They shouldn't be disappointed about that. But right now they still are. We're still too result-driven: a project has been completed, there are new lamp-posts, a few trees and a bench. Just like in the plan. But then it turns out people aren't sitting where they're supposed to be sitting but prefer the other side. My colleagues are sometimes too quick to see that as failure. That's not necessarily the case. In fact it's good. You learn with each other and you see an area starting to take shape. In that respect, Spoorzone is a unique living testing ground for urban development.'

TRANSFORMATION OF STATION AREA TURNS BREDA INTO HIP AND VIBRANT CITY

Challenging residents and users

You can still almost see the distaste in Bertwin van Rooijen's face. 'The area around the station,' says the programme manager of Via Breda, 'looked terrible. There was a great deal of derelict land with old railway tracks and grass growing in between them. The districts to the north of the railway line, which had suffered from the odour and noise for years, were also deteriorating badly.' We are sitting in Breda's city hall with Van Rooijen and communications consultant Peter Jeucken. On the table is a thick book with photos and drawings of Via Breda, the programme worth about 1 billion euros that radically changed the appearance of the station area.

From the onset, Breda viewed the new construction of the station as an opportunity to improve the coherence of the entire city. 'There's an area around the station that's as large as a city centre,' Van Rooijen says. 'It's essentially a second city. It was separated from the rest of the city by the railway line. We thought it was an excellent public space, which needed to be joined to the city. The station functioned as the driving force in the plans. That's why we deliberately gave it two faces.'

One driving force is not enough for such a large area. The municipality therefore designated a number of 'nodes' that would help to improve the area. One of them was the old canning factory. The municipality bought it and only allowed tenants to move in who were somehow associated with the cultural sector. It also determined that whoever performed community tasks, such as keeping the area clean, would pay less rent.

Functions for which there was no space in the old centre were designated to this area. There are many creative companies there now, for example, including a recording studio made out of straw and a small brewery. There's a skate park, Pier15 and an urban beach, Belcrum Beach, which is run entirely by volunteers. Everything takes place based on entrepreneurship or voluntarism: subsidies do not come into play here.

The area is far from being finished. Indeed, the municipality wants to build a water storage area on the grounds where the sugar factory once stood, because a great deal of water flows this way, from Belgium for example. Housing construction has not ended yet in the Havenkwartier either. Amvest intends to build another 300 apartments where three factories still stand.

Regional hub becomes pivotal point

The Via Breda programme has transformed Breda's station from a regional hub into a high-quality public transport terminal on the High Speed Line. This has made Breda a pivotal point between Antwerp/Brussels and Rotterdam/Amsterdam. The programme concerned a New Key Project: the State provided additional funds for good urban integration. This year the station was declared the most beautiful building in the Netherlands. Apartments were built in the station area, a courthouse is being developed, and an international hotel and business centre will be located here in the future. The districts in the station's vicinity have been addressed as well. Developments are still in full swing, particularly in the Havenkwartier. This area, about 10 hectares in size, used to accommodate large companies, such as a sugar factory and an iron foundry. Now space is being offered here for start-ups, the creative industry, recreation and residential housing. It was quite exceptional that users could go about their business free from the constraints of regulations, but also without subsidies.

It was quite exceptional that the municipality freed the Havenkwartier from the constraints of regulation. This entailed that residents and users, like good neighbours, could determine the rules of the game, as long as they were mindful of safety in the area. That was new for the users as well. '"How many decibels can we produce?" they would ask me,' recalls Van Rooijen. 'To which I would reply: "that's up to you. As long as you don't get into an argument with your neighbours." Then they immediately went and sounded out their neighbours.'

Many civil servants had to get used to the idea that the municipality was acting more as a process supervisor than a regulator. 'When we announced that we were going to free the area from the constraints of regulation,' Van Rooijen says, 'we received letters from public servants telling us that we were going to fail miserably!' 'But now,' Jeucken says, 'it has had a

knock-on effect. People are realising that something can also be successful if you abandon the traditional approach of ticking off the boxes and relinquish control.'

Via Breda has a complex mix of ingredients: a large area, a long-term initiative and many parties involved, such as the State, NS, ProRail and commercial developers. Nonetheless, the process unfolded more quickly than anticipated, says Van Rooijen. 'The fact that many functions were accommodated under one roof in the station, in which all parties were involved, was a unifying factor. Also, things tended to accelerate as soon as something tangible materialised. That happened during the economic crisis, of all times.'

The spatial results are impressive. Take the Havenkwartier, for example, which used to be a no-go area that you wouldn't be caught in after sundown. Now it's hip and vibrant. 'Recently I was at the Drie Hoefijzers, the former brewery,' Jeucken says. 'All of the outdoor cafés were packed. And last year there was an event about steam trains, organised by the inhabitants of Belcrum, which attracted thousands of people.'

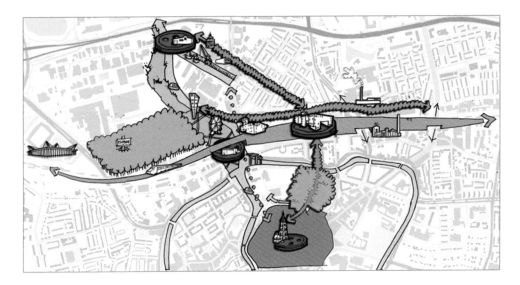

The districts to the north of the centre, Belcrum and Spoorbuurt, have also benefitted. Substantial investments were made in these districts' public space. This happened in a way that suits Breda, according to Van Rooijen and Jeucken. 'That means: restrained but using high-quality materials,' Van Rooijen says. 'We deployed sleek street profiles and stuck to the historical street layout, including thirty-metre-wide avenues lined by trees. We didn't want it to resemble an amusement park, with something different every few metres. That's a culture we have adhered to for at least thirty years here when designing public space.'

The area in the immediate vicinity of the station is attracting many private investors. The prices per square metre here are the highest in the city and have reached the level of cities such as Amsterdam, The Hague, Rotterdam and Utrecht. Is that a good thing? Yes, both Van Rooijen and Jeucken nod their head in agreement. They point out that American companies are already establishing their headquarters here, which is bound to have a positive effect on employment.

Belcrum, which not long ago was a district in decline, is now one of the most dynamic districts in the Netherlands in terms of homes sold. Referring to Belcrum Beach, real estate agents are using terms such as 'living by a beach' in their advertisements.

There's plenty of economic and cultural activity in other words. But the most important impact that Via Breda has had is perhaps a psychological one, according to the two

men. 'Breda has regained its pride,' Jeucken says. 'Even city residents who don't see the station's appeal say: it has made special things happen.' 'From an exuberant provincial town that people left to move to Amsterdam and Rotterdam, we are becoming a pulsating city that serves a larger region and which is unifying people again,' Van Rooijen says.

But both men warn against becoming complacent. 'We must continue to focus on added value,' Van Rooijen says. 'If you don't, there's the danger that it will become a dormitory suburb. You have to ensure that you always have a viable driving force. And you have to keep stimulating and challenging entrepreneurs. For example, let them contribute to the refurbishment of buildings too. Our task is to have a strict selection procedure. If a candidate says "I don't need to do it for the money," then he's out. That kind of attitude is always lethal in a project like this.'

DO:

– Make sure your plan is not watertight – have the courage to make it exciting for yourself too

DON'T:

– Control, dominate or restrict

THE METAMORPHOSIS OF SLOTERDIJK

It's no coincidence that the conversation takes place at Bret, a bar/restaurant that does a lot with beer and is housed in red sea containers in front of Sloterdijk Station. 'Bret' refers both to the nearby nature area and a special kind of brewer's yeast.

Bret is only one of the many improvements that have been made to the area around Sloterdijk Station, which until recently was considered dismal. A piece on the website upcoming.nl artfully and hilariously tore the station and its surroundings to shreds: 'Even a burnt-out Fiat Panda looks more inviting than interior and exterior of Sloterdijk Station,' it read.

'If you had no business going there, you wouldn't go at all,' agrees Pien van der Ploeg, communication consultant in area development at the municipality of Amsterdam. When, on top of all that, the offices around the station started emptying out during the economic crisis – some new buildings never even had a tenant before being converted into hotels – the municipality decided to intervene. 'We wanted to prevent the area from deteriorating,' says Arwen Schram, project manager of the team tasked with area development at Sloterdijk. 'Moreover, we didn't think that single-purpose office areas were of this time anymore.'

A strategy paper was released, followed by a flexible zoning plan, which allowed for the construction of hotels and housing in the area. 'The project team saw the potential of the area, but also realised that a great deal had to happen before others would recognise it too. So our reasoning was: instead

of first allocating the plots and only then tackling the public space, we should do it the other way around,' Van der Ploeg says. 'Our strategy was based on the idea that you have to put cost before benefit. That was quite bold, because it happened during a time of major cutbacks.'

An estate agent for the area was called in and asked users what they needed. Van der Ploeg explains how it unfolded. 'Do you want a safe pedestrian crossing? Okay, we'll take care of it. A bench where staff can eat a sandwich at lunchtime? Deal. Those were quick wins. In addition, the team organised symposiums with companies about the future of the area. There was a lot of enthusiasm for that, except with the foreign property owners, because for them you're nothing more than a column in a spreadsheet.'

After the strategy paper and the accompanying zoning plan were developed, the municipality was the first to start working on the station's square, Orlyplein. This occurred in co-creation with the owners and users of the square. The abandoned bus station became an oasis of green, art and light. The way the footpaths came about was special. 'In December,' Van der Ploeg recalls, 'the designers got together. It had just been snowing, so there were footprints all over the square. The designers used these footprints as a blueprint for the footpaths in between the green areas.'

Part of the strategy for the area was to make it a more attractive place to be. Placemaking was a key aspect of this. For example, there were festivals on unoccupied plots and even in empty offices. Temporary beach chairs and a life-size chess board appeared on Orlyplein. Van der Ploeg took steps of her own as well. She managed to install the largest Christmas tree in Amsterdam in 2015. With the help of the owner of the 95-metre-high Crystal Tower she stuck cardboard panels on the windows of this office building, creating a gigantic lit-up Christmas tree.

The temporary facilities were also essential to making this an attractive place to be. The bar/restaurant pavilion Bret is one example, as is the padel club (padel is a racket sport), which will be opening its doors in late 2017. In agreement with the municipality, Bret launched 'De Tuin van Bret', or Bret's Garden, on an undeveloped piece of land opposite the bar/restaurant pavilion, which included a vineyard, among other things, surrounded by facilities. It too was constructed of red sea containers.

The transformation strategy had a positive effect in terms of arousing the interest of hotels owners in particular. They came to the area in droves in the period following the crisis. There are now nine hotels with about 2,000 beds in the immediate vicinity of Sloterdijk, one of which has the shape of old train carriages. As office space was transformed into hotels, the municipal transformation managers were always sure to give the surroundings important consideration. They were also involved in allocating uses for the plinths and determining the appearance of the façades. 'Their discussions went something like this: if we build a more attractive street, will you fix up the façade?' says Arwen Schram.

After the hotel owners came the developers. Many in fact. The first tender for a housing plot, which was released in September 2016, elicited as many as 21 responses from developers. There is space for about 1,500 apartments in the coming five years, a number which will increase to a maximum of 7,500. The municipality is using the tender not only to influence the nature of the construction, but also that of the environment. Indeed, the award criteria specify that the plinths must contain cultural facilities, cafés and restaurants, or recreational facilities, so that they contribute to a lively commercial and residential environment. Quality and sustainability carry the most weight in awarding the tender. Heijmans has won the battle for the first plot with a type of 'urban green living' that is striking for its abundant green space, even in the high-rise.

Although placemaking was a consideration during the processes of transformation, new housing construction and public space redevelopment, it still remains a focus in its

Hotels replacing offices

Sloterdijk has existed as a village since the fourteenth century. At the time, it was surrounded by farms. From 1890 onwards, it had its own station on the first railway system in the Netherlands, which linked Amsterdam to Haarlem. In the 1980s, when Sloterdijk became part of Amsterdam, a new, high-tech station was built. Three railway lines converged there: the one to Haarlem, the one to Den Helder and the one to Schiphol Airport. The metro stopped there as well. At the end of the last century, it became home to a business park called Amsterdam Teleport. As a result of rapid developments in ICTs (internet) and the real estate crisis, this particular function never really got off the ground. Currently, the station area consists mainly of offices. The municipality has announced its intention of improving the area's quality of life and increasing its diversity.

own right. 'When things were so difficult for this area, we welcomed
much of what came our way,' Schram says. 'Now that we've moved
forward, the team can be more selective.' Temporary initiatives are no
longer accepted. But a budget has been earmarked for placemaking
in the long term. A community-building process is ongoing, in which
the municipality is participating. The idea is to have the community
eventually develop their own initiatives that dovetail with the final
blueprint: a cool and appealing area to live and work.

The significance of the developments at Sloterdijk has increased now
that the municipality has launched another project called Haven-Stad,
which will transform former port areas just to the north of Sloterdijk
and generate 40,000 to 70,000 apartments and 45,000 to 58,000
jobs. In the meantime, in addition to the housing construction and
the related facilities at Sloterdijk, there are other improvements that
could be made. For example, the connection to neighbouring districts
could be better, and the station itself could use an overhaul. 'But
tourists already see this as a typical Amsterdam area, with all its
bicycles parked outside,' Van der Ploeg says. 'In fact, they don't see
Orlyplein as square but as a station park. As far as I'm concerned,
though, this can only be called a success if the city's inhabitants
embrace Sloterdijk as a genuine piece of Amsterdam.'

DO'S:
– Be open to outside initiatives. Involve the area's owners and users,
  as they have the expertise of experience. Look differently at what
  you already have: an empty office building can also be a place to
  hold a festival or create a mega-Christmas tree.

DON'T:
– Always keep the final blueprint in mind, so that you can use it as a
  litmus test for new initiatives. If they don't improve the place,
  it's better to decline.

SPOORZONE TILBURG: IN THE FOOTSTEPS OF THE KING AND QUEEN

The king and the queen relished the prospect on King's Day 2017 to roam through Tilburg's slightly rough and hip railway zone: Spoorzone. Steps were quickly built so that the royal couple could walk from Spoorzone to the city centre without any difficulty. Until 2013, Spoorzone was a hidden area. A barrier right in the middle of the city. 'The area was totally walled in, and residents from the north of Tilburg had to go around the area to reach the centre,' says Anouk Thijssen, programme manager of Spoorzone. 'Now there are people coming and going from the northern part of the city to the centre and vice versa.'

Anyone following the king and queen's footsteps will arrive in a large area right next to the railway. The area has various beautiful and historical buildings with evocative names, such as the woodshed, the polygonal shed, the forge and the locomotive hall. Spoorzone is a former marshalling yard and workshop with a surface area of 75 hectares. From east to west, the area is 1.5 kilometres long and consists of three sub-areas: the former grounds of Van Gend & Loos, the western flank and the former NS workshop. Today, it is part of the city's cultural-industrial heritage.

Anouk Thijssen takes us along to the area. 'Only six months
ago, the intention was to demolish all the old buildings
in this area. That's hardly imaginable now. Luckily it was
decided to preserve many of those buildings. The province
decided, in late 2015, to grant a subsidy of 3.5 million euros
for the preservation of cultural heritage and was therefore
an important partner for the municipality.' The Council
agreed to keep the existing buildings. This meant that a
significant number of square metres could no longer be
developed as was foreseen in earlier plans, and therefore
the properties had to be written off. The total amount
came to 19.4 million euros.

Anouk is enthusiastic about the development of the area.
'The municipality is investing in a knowledge economy
combined with housing. It will take at least ten more years
until the area is completely ready. We chose to invest
immediately in good connections so that the people of Tilburg
could explore the area. The investment for infrastructure was
highlighted in the development plans. A new road connecting
east to west called the Nieuwe Burgemeester Brokxlaan was
built, as well as a number of side streets that connect the
northern part of Tilburg to the centre. One of these roads,

the Willem II passage, runs under a building and railway line. The new station's underpass also creates a connection from the south to the north side that wasn't there before. The new area only opened last year, but people have wasted no time discovering it.'

The existing buildings have been given temporary functions, such as events and the Hall of Fame, a large skate park that attracts young people from all over the surroundings of Tilburg. The woodshed accommodates a beautifully renovated building with a hip and popular restaurant and offices. The 'Kennismakerij' is a precursor of the 'new-style library', which will be opened next year in the restored Lochal (the locomotive hall), together with workshops and an art counter. 'We receive weekly telephone calls and e-mails from people that would like to temporarily settle in Spoorzone. At this point, we need to disappoint them. All of the premises are being used.' Important future users of the area include Tilburg University, Fontys Hogescholen, ROC Tilburg and the Persgroep, as well as the editorial board of the daily *Brabants Dagblad*. Together with the municipality, they developed 'Mind Labs': a hotspot in the area of interactive technology and behaviour. They are set to occupy a building together. The parties are so enthusiastic about the new partnership that they don't want to wait for the new-build and have decided to move to a temporarily renovated building in Spoorzone in late 2017, right across from the station.

'The more the area is developed, the more the functions will merge into each other, which will make it difficult to maintain those functions that exist today. If offices and housing will be introduced here, they won't be compatible with the organisation of big festivals, for example, because of noise pollution. But the nice thing about it is that new concepts and new kinds of partnerships arise from this kind of endeavour. The apparent contradiction between a raw and creative character, on the one hand, and convenience and modern solutions, on the other, coexists well here. In that sense, the Tilburg Spoorzone is a real hotspot, an innovative art factory with opportunities for everyone.

'In the framework of the city's official strategy for the city centre in the 21st century, we had several talks with entrepreneurs. For example, we met with the people from the skate park to talk about how they viewed their future. After that, we examined what kind of housing and what kind of location is most suitable for them. This is how we turn things around. The advice from entrepreneurs in the city is to keep some parts of the city purposely cluttered and make sure that not all of the areas are so cleanly developed. That could be in Spoorzone or in another location in Tilburg.'

DOS:

- Invest immediately in infrastructure, such as roads and public areas, so that the area appeals from the word go. Highlight this investment in your plans.
- Connect areas, such as the Willem II underpass in Tilburg.
- Ensure as a municipality that you maintain sufficient influence on a given area's development. That can be achieved by keeping land holdings and gradually selling them. Market players have different interests than municipalities.
- Bind strategic partners to your location. For example, attract a library or knowledge institute to your area. These are the (future) ambassadors of your area development.

DON'T:

- Engage in a long-term contract with a developer based on a blueprint of an area. That makes you less flexible when it comes to dealing with changing perceptions.

AS AN AREA DEVELOPER, WE FACILITATE PLACEMAKING

All players in area development are important for increasing value

Increasingly, area developer BPD Ontwikkeling BV is organising activities to attract people to a location before it's even clear how the area is going to be developed. It's an enormous change, stresses development manager Rosalie de Boer and area marketer Hans-Hugo Smit: 'We used to put a fence around this kind of area and no one was allowed in.'

'In 2006-2007, area developer BPD Ontwikkeling BV bought a large portion of the industrial estate called De Binckhorst in The Hague in order to develop a large-scale and especially a top-down masterplan with the municipality and one investor,' BPD area marketer Hans-Hugo Smit explains. 'But the crisis intervened, which made the transformation seem infeasible, and ultimately we got rid of a large portion of the property again. We rented out the buildings in a few of the remaining locations in a kind of anti-squat agreement.'

A few years ago, the municipality launched new plans to develop De Binckhorst into a residential and work area. 'Of course we wanted to share our thoughts about how we could contribute to its development,' Smit says. 'The Kompaan brewery was at one of our locations, which is something they were aware of. Their activities were responsible for attracting many people to the area. That gave us the idea to do more

with our property. But we had no idea who was at this other location because an external party was managing the lettings.'

'We went by and asked them if we could have a look inside,' adds his colleague, development manager Rosalie de Boer. 'It turned out that many musicians who mean a great deal to the music scene in The Hague and in the Netherlands had set up studio and practice spaces there. We then commissioned ANNA Vastgoed & Cultuur to come up with ideas on how to use this local asset. Together with them, we organised a brainstorm with the musicians to find ways of giving this place added value, using the musicians as the starting point.'

The plan for the Pollux Studio arose from that. 'We discovered that there's a huge network affiliated with these musicians,' De Boer says, 'including writers, producers, graphic designers, and so on. At that point, ANNA decided to pitch everyone in the music scene that wanted to set themselves up there and had something to contribute to the buildings *and* to the area.'

'This is really something special for us,' Smit says. 'We're area developers. We want to develop real estate, that's how we make our living. Now we're investing in the area even though we have no idea whether we're going to do something with it, and if so what.

You could say that in the worst-case scenario at least there's a social return, but of course our organisation can't operate purely on that. What it's really all about is combining the commercial with the social.'

'There definitely has to be a business case,' De Boer stresses. 'For this kind of project to last, it has to ultimately be able to pay its own way and not rely on subsidies. Taking on ANNA Vastgoed & Cultuur is a one-off investment that won't repay itself. That's our contribution to the area as an area developer, but after that initial investment the revenue from the lettings has to offset the management costs. 'And,' Smit adds, 'this is how we highlight the area's benefits, which increases the value of the real estate.'

De Boer: 'For me it's primarily a strategy to highlight an area for future residents, entrepreneurs and visitors. In order to make placemaking last in the long term, you need parties such as ANNA Vastgoed & Cultuur, the municipality and the people themselves.' Smit concurs: 'We're the driving force, but a chain of placemakers is needed to eventually own the process.'

Another example of placemaking is Proeftuin Erasmusveld, situated in the green strip between the south-west of The Hague and Wateringse Veld. 'The municipality wants this to become the most sustainable district in the city,' Smit says. 'That provides us with the opportunity to present a unique proposition at the interface of ecology and collective interests. That's why we started to think about what we could do to instil that in potential residents' minds at an early stage.'

'During the first phase, we launched a design competition,' De Boer says. 'The assignment was: incorporate the core values of this project, "Healthy, Urban and Living Together", into a design for this area. We chose the best entries from over 60,000. That's a very different way of approaching the development of an area than we're used to.'

Ultimately, BPD wants to build approximately 350 new housing units on Erasmusveld. While designing has begun for the first 100 houses on one side of the plot, in the framework of placemaking BPD has launched the Proeftuin Erasmusveld urban field and a tiny houses project on the other side of the plot.

'These could be two completely separate developments, but the trick is to bring these two together,' De Boer explains. 'Our Sales department, for example, is used to receiving drawings at a certain point, then launching a website, after which they start to sell the houses. Now the activities that we're organising in a given place are generating a database of 1,000 addresses of interested parties before sales have even begun. As a result, it's easier for them to do their work and it's in their economic interest. That's a good incentive.'

Connecting is the magic word, in more sense than one. 'Everything you do costs money,' Smit says, 'including organic things. If you want to build an urban garden out of idealistic motives but don't have the money to invest in it, then you can look for commercial partners who may seem at first sight to clash with your ideals. I think you need to find a way to connect, without betraying yourself. That holds true for us as well. We had to be willing to promise that we wouldn't touch the land destined for the urban garden for 2.5 years. It's true that we pay Suzanne, the woman who manages the urban field, but she does put a great deal of love and energy into it, and so she has to be able to trust us not to tell her, after a month or two: it's been fun, but now we need to build here.'

An example of the cross-fertilisation that he is referring to recently took place when Smit attended a meeting with business partners at the urban field. 'Suzanne didn't attend the meeting but did bring us a box of zucchinis. So all these business people went home with two zucchinis under their arms. These small gestures create more understanding for each other.'

'Or take that couple from Groningen,' De Boer says in agreement, 'who saw what was happening here on the website for the urban garden. They've come by three times already and may well move here one day. When I tell colleagues about them, they react totally surprised. But what we're doing has simply generated a different kind of energy.'

'And ultimately more revenue too,' Smit says. 'There's a buzz at the moment. We're getting recognition through the publication of articles in local papers and so on. There's no way we would have succeeded on this scale with a construction sign and a fence around the area.'

DOS:

- Be willing to understand other people's points of view.
- Approach it professionally, that will make it sustainable.
- View placemaking from the perspective of a chain of partners (and not one partner that does everything)

DON'TS:

- Don't decide top-down what should be built without looking at what's already there first.
- Don't take over the communication from the placemakers; it's their narrative. Our only job is to facilitate.

CLUB RHIJNHUIZEN IS THE PERFECT EXAMPLE OF MAKING YOUR OWN LUCK

Developers and users both spend free time and money for placemaking in Nieuwegein

How do you transform an 80-hectare office area with 100 different owners into a residential-business area that will entice the people of Utrecht to leave their city? Led by location marketer Emilie Vlieger and public developer and STIPO partner Hans Karssenberg, Club Rhijnhuizen in Nieuwegein is well on its way to making this miracle happen.

In 2015 the municipality of Nieuwegein approached a number of parties to start thinking about the development of Rijnhuizen, a business park 80 hectares large which, with 100 owners, had become an extremely fragmented property plagued by vacancy. Most of the buildings were in the possession of local owners/ users that occupied one office building with its surrounding grounds. The park was built next to the old village of Jutphaas and consisted, with the exception of a handful of original residents and a secondary school, of mirror glass offices from the 1980s.

The municipality wanted to deal with the vacancy problem by transforming the area into a residential-business area, but how do you go about that when there are so many different owners? The municipality agreed with the owners that they needed to find an area manager that would be responsible for both designing and promoting the area.

Location marketer Emilie Vlieger from Vliegerprojecten and public developer Hans Karssenberg were both asked to make a pitch for the assignment. After the presentations, someone said: actually you both complement each other well. Why don't you do this together? 'That was well spotted,' Karssenberg says. 'A superb idea. Emilie focuses more on the location marketing and I focus on the area development and financial strategy.'

'We immediately organised a kick-off meeting for owners, entrepreneurs and stakeholders, Vlieger says. 'At the meeting we told the group what we expected from them: that we would all develop this area together. We made a presentation about the history of the area and about its special places, such as the oldest fort in the Dutch Water Line and the Rijnhuizen Castle, which is a listed monument. At that first meeting, we already started drawing in patios on a map.'

One of the companies made a space available for future meetings, called it the clubhouse, *et voilà*: Club Rhijnhuizen was born.

The municipality indicated it wanted to invest in the area management for half a year. 'So it was important to find a way in which all parties in whose interest it was to improve the area

could contribute to the financing of the Club. That's why we set up a cooperative consisting of the owners, developers and residents. We also agreed with the municipality that the Club would receive 10% of the contributions to the area that developers are obliged to give to the municipality to improve the area.'

One of Club Rhijnhuizen's tasks is to promote the area. 'Nieuwegein doesn't have a good reputation,' Vlieger explains, 'even though it's green here, there are special places and it's close to Utrecht. We want people in the surroundings to realise this and head this way. To show them everything that there is to see here, we organised activities with the Club such as Heritage Day, historical walks, cycling tours and this year, for the first time, the Rijnhuizen Run, a 5 km run through the area.'

Vlieger and Karssenberg were quick to conclude that placemaking stood to generate massive gains, because at the start you couldn't walk around the fort as sheep grazed there, there were no meeting places and the infrastructure was geared towards heavy goods traffic instead of families with children.

'Together with the club members and the municipality, the Club has now decided that the area needs to have 10 "really great places",' Karssenberg says. 'We don't know where yet. It's an organic area development, so we're monitoring places that are the first to prove themselves to be dynamic. We started a placegame in which we examined the criteria needed for a good place. What do we want here? Some good ideas came out of that, such as a swing for two at the most romantic place by the water, a playground and information signs about the fort.'

After the workshop, a 'pleasant place' team was set up that managed to secure some grants. Three months later, the first steps had been taken, and new, wilder ideas emerged. For example, the team is now testing the waters to find out whether the fort watchman's house can be made available for free to artists, so that they can provide programming in return.

Another example is a large, green area where Kondor Wessels and BPD are set to launch a project in two years' time. 'In the meantime, we want to use the land to bring attention to the area in a different way, Karssenberg says. 'We held a contest, and the winner is now going to create temporary green workplaces there and the largest Tiny Houses village in the Netherlands. Kondor Wessels and BPD are fully involved in this. The fact that developers can get together with existing stakeholders and secure funding for placemaking is unique.'

Club Rhijnhuizen now has 260 members, and interest in the area has increased dramatically. 'In the first year, we had a handful of interested people,' Karssenberg says, 'but at this point I'm showing a

new developer around every week, and there are barely any plots left where something isn't already happening. Of course, we've also had a windfall in that the housing market in Utrecht went up as much as it did, but it's also the result of the recognition we've received from industry, as well as the Club's tremendous energy.'

The extent of the impact was evident when Rijnhuizen Castle was at risk of being sold to a Chinese property developer, who wanted to build offices and residences in the back garden. 'We were extremely disheartened by this development,' Karssenberg says, 'because the castle is one of the most beautiful parts of the area. We expressed our concern during one of the club evenings, which is how Ubbo Hylkema, former director of the State Monument Preservation Agency of the Netherlands, heard about it. He's extremely enthusiastic about what we're doing here. That's why he informed his brother-in-law, who had just sold his energy company, about the castle. And that's how it happened. Now we're talking with him about the possibility of opening the garden to the public so it can become part of the park. A nice example of how, as a Club, you can make your own luck.'

SOCIALLY RELEVANT PLACEMAKING IN THE WETENSCHAPPERSBUURT

What does placemaking really mean? This question arose spontaneously at the table when the parties first met at ERA Contour. 'Nowadays it all too often means: we're going to develop something; so what can we do in the meantime?' says chairwoman Bianca Seekles. 'It comes down to making a place hip,' adds Edward van Dongen, head of Initiative & Concept. 'But we have a broader view of placemaking,' adds Seekles.

They both consider their approach to the Wetenschappersbuurt a good example of such a 'broad' placemaking vision. 'We were adamant,' Van Dongen says, 'about including residents in the development of the plans. When you talk to people in this kind of neighbourhood you primarily get negative comments about the municipality and the housing corporation. We had to find out what they *really* wanted. Based on the idea that children are less inhibited and biased, we started to take walks through the neighbourhood with students from Group 8 (11 to 12 years old) of the primary school *De Peperklip*. Later on, we also conducted a workshop with the Schiedam Children's Council.'

It emerged that the way children experience liveability and safety differs greatly from adults. Among other things, they pointed out that the green areas were situated too far on the periphery of the district. And that even though some places were attractive the children didn't want to play there because some weird, drunken man was always sitting there on a bench.

'We shared our findings with the residents: that's what your children are saying,' explains Van Dongen. 'This immediately created a positive vibe and made the Liveability Barometer's score rise considerably, even before a spade was put into the ground.'

'That's what genuine interest can bring about. Obviously that had been lacking before,' according to Seekles.

The responses from the municipality and the housing corporation Woonplus, which owns most of the rental units in the Wetenschappersbuurt, were positive as well. In fact, so positive that they were willing to abandon their customary approach, which entailed working on the basis of a detailed, pre-established urban development plan. 'Our creativity sparked their creativity as well,' Seekles notes with satisfaction.

The Wetenschappersbuurt

The *Wetenschappersbuurt* (literally the Scientist's District) is a neighbourhood in the east of Schiedam comprising some 400 housing units of pre-war and post-war construction. The district had gradually become impoverished, rundown and unsafe. The Wetenschappersbuurt received a score of 'highly inadequate' on the Liveability Barometer, the worst possible rating. Initially, the municipality and the housing corporation wanted to demolish all rental flats and replace them with single-family dwellings, while retaining the existing street layout and building lines. The planning process involved spacemaker ERA Contour, housing corporation *Woonplus* and residents, and ultimately led to unexpected outcomes.

The children were also involved in choosing the architect. And this, too, led to an unexpected result. 'The architects had to pay extra special attention to the way they presented their story,' Van Dongen says. 'Two did it perfectly. The third one might have had the best plan but didn't know how to communicate it effectively.'

The process created a strong feeling of team spirit. 'The residents' underdog mindset diminished when they felt that they really mattered,' Van Dongen explains. 'And that, in turn, had an impact on the civil servants. They started to view the residents as a source of creativity rather than troublemakers. We had the good fortune of dealing with people, both at the municipality and the housing corporation, who showed a genuine interest in the project. The whole process depends a great deal on people.'

All residents had the opportunity to provide input. And they did. For instance, they challenged the type of construction. They wanted to retain two apartment buildings, partly because the planned number of housing units decreased from 400 to 200 and residents didn't receive a return guarantee. 'That caused heated discussions. We ultimately kept the two apartment buildings, for both urban planning and social reasons,' says Van Dongen.

Some parties submitted different zoning suggestions. Residents, for example, argued that a road across the canal had little added value in terms of traffic and should therefore be replaced with a

for cyclists and pedestrians. 'If we had raised that issue with the municipality, we would have received a negative response,' claims Van Dongen. 'But the fact that the residents brought up this issue made it different.' He's already dreaming of having the children design the little bridge.

Planning for the Wetenschappersbuurt began four years ago. The first new housing units have already been delivered. Construction is being carried out in phases and will be completed in 2020. Seekles and Van Dongen think that the process has been remarkably swift, despite the fact that nothing much happened in the first year and a half from a spatial planning point of view. 'Things that usually slow down a process, e.g. endless consultations with the neighbourhood, actually worked as an accelerator because it helped eliminate resistance,' Seekles says.

Seekles and Van Dongen believe that their approach is of 'great social relevance'. 'Eventually we're going to have to deal with a wave of housing estates built in the sixties and seventies,' Van Dongen says. 'This will serve as a lesson. However, each place is different and requires an individual approach; you can't achieve every goal by consulting with children. So far, we've not repeated this method.'

Placemaking is an ongoing process. After all, the situation in a neighbourhood keeps changing constantly. Seekles and Van Dongen don't rule out that more expensive rental units will be added in the future. This is attributable to the success of the first sales: the housing units sold like hot cakes. Buyers were primarily social risers from the neighbourhood, for whom a suitable dwelling was not available. 'You develop along with a neighbourhood. Plans aren't carved in stone, where nothing is possible once they've been established,' says Seekles.

The residents are also expected to keep contributing to the placemaking idea. Seekles and Van Dongen have in mind the Mediterranean quarter Le Medi, developed by ERA Contour, as an example. 'Someone built a small shed there at some point,' Seekles recalls. 'Instead of quarrelling, the residents got together to discuss the matter and agreed on the height and colour of the sheds. This can only succeed if people have a say in their living environment from the onset, and are not just confronted with a fait accompli.'

Do the two feel like placemakers? 'Yes,' replies Seekles. 'We applied all facets of the placemaking concept in the Wetenschappersbuurt, both from a social and spatial viewpoint. And we didn't need to apply that trick of creating something hip and cool.'

'Many designers are convinced of their autonomously designed plans,' Van Dongen says. 'But this way of designing doesn't work in

vulnerable areas. It doesn't make a difference there whether you think something is beautiful or ugly; what matters is that it's good and suitable.'

DO:

– Keep car traffic as close to the boulevard as possible. Try to intercept cars as early as possible and ensure that there are good facilities for public transport and slow traffic. Remain open to possibilities. Study the place and the people who live there, enter into discussions with them and use the findings as the basis for your plans.

DON'T:

– Keep car traffic as close to the boulevard as possible. Try to intercept cars as early as possible and ensure that there are good facilities for public transport and slow traffic. Don't get into a defensive mode if an idea is rejected. Don't make promises you can't keep (but do live up to your promises).

PLACEMAKERS IN ARNHEM SEARCH FOR (AND FIND) RHINEGOLD

A better connection between city and Rhine – that's why Arnhem decided to try placemaking. The city is engaged in large-scale placemaking and is putting major emphasis on communication and collaboration.

Arnhem, a city that currently has 150,000 inhabitants, was founded in the Middle Ages on the Jansbeek, a stream flowing from the hills of the Veluwe to the Rhine. The stream's hydropower was used to operate the paper mills that drove Arnhem's development in those days.

For centuries the Rhine flowed a few kilometres south of the city. In 1530 the river's course was diverted northwards so a toll could be levied. When Arnhem grew in later years, the Rhine essentially became the city's rear side. Urban sprawl in the 21st century took place primarily south of the Rhine. Apart from being the city's rear side, the river also became a barrier between the northern and southern city districts.

One of Arnhem's foremost ambitions is to make better use of the Rhine's huge potential (the Rhinegold) and to turn the river into a link rather than a barrier. That's a huge task because the river banks are some 15 kilometres long. Arnhem therefore opted for a gradual approach that accorded placemaking a prominent role.

In recent decades emphasis was placed primarily on connecting the inner city with the Rhine. The accent is now shifting to the river banks opposite and on both sides of the city centre.

The aim of placemaking is to create fertile ground for future developments, both small-scale temporary projects and long-term area developments. Arnhem is not proceeding on the basis of a rigidly defined plan, but has opted for the process of placemaking. In addition to concrete placemaking activities, this also comprises the establishment of a network and communication trajectory.

A Rhine Group has been set up, comprised of parties associated with the Rhine. They all have Arnhem's interests at heart. This group includes project developers, a rowing club, creative entrepreneurs, cultural institutions and the municipality, among others. The group meets several times a year to share information and to brainstorm. The idea is that the group's large network can lobby effectively for a better connection between Arnhem and the Rhine. What's more, it gives the participating parties a chance to be actively involved in placemaking.

Communication is another important pillar. It can make a broad public aware of the beauty of the river and all the possibilities it

offers for a variety of activities. The Rhine Group and its network use social media to publicise what's happening along the Rhine. Many communications are of a personal nature, such as videos from Arnhem residents involved in recreational activities on and around the river.

Arnhem has a relatively large number of creative entrepreneurs who organise cultural activities and festivals. They're at the heart of placemaking along the Rhine. The municipality supports their initiatives with subsidies and uncomplicated licensing procedures. That results in more and more reasons for spending time along the river banks.

Many events have been organised along the river in the past years, such as a quayside market, quayside days, city beaches, a circus theatre and several festivals. Moreover, during the summer months there is a ferry service between the city centre and *Stadsblokken*, the green heart on the opposite side.

These activities have changed the mindset of residents and visitors. In the past, the river was hard to find and uninviting, but nowadays increasingly more people come to the river banks for recreational activities. Slowly the river is connecting Arnhem North with Arnhem South.

The old function of the Rhine Quay is coming back to life during the annual quayside days. Visitors can admire magnificent old ships, steam and other ship engines, and learn about maritime crafts such as sail making, net mending and rope splicing. The city also received a historical harbour crane as a gift, which occupies a prominent place on the lower quay.

Quayside markets were organised several times a year and the area between the two Rhine bridges became a kilometre long flea market. Residents sold special goods at those markets, and visitors could enjoy live music and cultural acts. And since a few years, a hospitality establishment has been operating a successful city beach on the lower quay.

Part of the Stadsblokken area will be transformed into green festival grounds in the future. In the meantime, several cultural events are already being held there every year. *Festival De Luie Hond* and *Cirque de la Liberté* are attractive examples of events that create a link with the water. The river provides a magnificent setting. Since these activities draw large numbers of people, they get to see the city from another perspective. Indeed, Arnhem looks quite different viewed from Stadsblokken and reveals a unique urban character, something that was only known to 'the happy few' until recently.

The plans are to build a historic harbour in the area. A small hospitality pavilion with a workplace is already operating in anticipation of the harbour's construction. There will be a ferry service between the city centre and Stadsblokken during the summer. The ferry will also help to ensure that the Rhine doesn't divide but connects.

The experiences with placemaking in Arnhem have been very positive so far. The initiatives and activities draw Arnhem's residents to the Rhine and bring the river and the city together. An atmosphere has been created that is conducive to collaboration, adventure, ambition and fun.

The city of Arnhem believes that placemaking has created a location where people enjoy staying, which previously was not the case. Placemaking has revealed the qualities of an area with potential. It lures people there and enables them to experience a formerly undiscovered spot: sometimes still slightly rough and industrial, but always authentic and with a touch of adventure. Placemaking lets you look at a city with fresh eyes. It's a harbinger of something new and radiates the energy of a city that moves forward.

EVERYONE CAN CLAIM THEIR OWN SPOT

How the Scheveningen boulevard reflects the city's international ambitions

Serving all of the users of the Scheveningen boulevard everywhere, all the time, is wishful thinking. But it's actually not necessary, says urban developer and area coordinator at the municipality of The Hague, Demet Voûte: 'Everyone has their own spot, even though as a municipality we didn't specifically plan it that way. Nor should we want to, in my opinion. These kinds of things take care of themselves.'

In 2015, the municipality of The Hague launched its 'Healthy Coast' project, the main aim of which was to bring back that seaside feeling in the public space. The project consisted, on the one hand, of making the public space in the beach area by the pier clean, safe and cohesive, and, on the other hand, of renovating the boulevard step by step.

'The Spanish architect Manuel de Solà-Morales designed the part between Sea Life and the harbour,' explains Demet Voûte, urban developer and area coordinator at the municipality of The Hague. 'Now that the South Boulevard is finished, it's suddenly clear how worn-down the area around the Kurhaus is. The Hague is the international city of peace and justice. There are many international organisations here, and we want to use the power of the landscape to enhance the city's appeal. Creating the conditions for new organisations to settle here starts with

the design. Everything has to be right. Take accessibility, for example: it takes too long to get to the boulevard. Public transport has to be improved, as does access for slow traffic. We have to intercept cars much earlier. We're working on an ambitious plan to achieve that.'

Redeveloping the boulevard is undoubtedly a complex task, among other reasons because the users are so diverse: expats have very different wishes than tourists or the people living behind the boulevard. Nevertheless, that's not an insurmountable problem, according to Voûte: 'When it's finished, it does of course have to be based on one design, but it will have many area-specific characteristics. The beach area of Scheveningen near the pier, for example, is extremely touristy with attractions such as the Kurhaus and, in the near future, Legoland. You won't find the average city resident there. They prefer to hang out on Zuiderstrand, Kijkduin or at Scheveningen Harbour. That's where people do their sports, and they, in turn, attract a crowd that likes to belong to and check out the scene. There's a much different, much more relaxed vibe there. The middle part of the boulevard is a kind of transition zone where there are fewer cafés and restaurants, and where the panoramic vistas invite people to walk and stroll around. Zwarte Pad has more of an Ibiza flavour to it. So everyone can claim their own spot, even though as a municipality we didn't specifically plan it that way. Nor should we want to, in my opinion. These kinds of things take care of themselves, as long as the design gives you the space to claim your spot.'

On the north side, for example, you regularly come across 'stepping stones', places where children can play, where there's a bench to sit on, or a spot where there's something worthwhile for tourists to take a picture of. 'The stairs with the sculptures, for example,' Voûte says, 'that has really become a great playground for children.' Other stepping stones are going to be placed in the vicinity of the Kurhaus, which is going to be renovated in nineteenth-century style, near the stairs to the pier and at the end of the boulevard. 'A large pavilion will be built there with international appeal. Anyone wanting to make an iconic picture of Scheveningen in the future, will take a photo of that.'

The basic idea underlying the design is that everyone must be able to find an agreeable place to be on the coast. 'It's typical of The Hague,' Voûte says. 'We're a large, international city consisting of all kinds of separate neighbourhoods with their own personality. The fact that not everything appeals to everyone is fine, but there does have to be some cohesion, and it's important that no one feels left out. The design of the boulevard plays a key role in that respect. The current boulevard is straight, but soon it will become curved, in line with the ideas of Solà-Morales. Before he made his design, Solà-Morales carried out a cultural-historical analysis to discover what would suit Scheveningen/The Hague. One of the things that it revealed was that the coastline used to have beautiful bends in it. To bring back these cultural-historical elements we need to revisit the spirit of the place. The

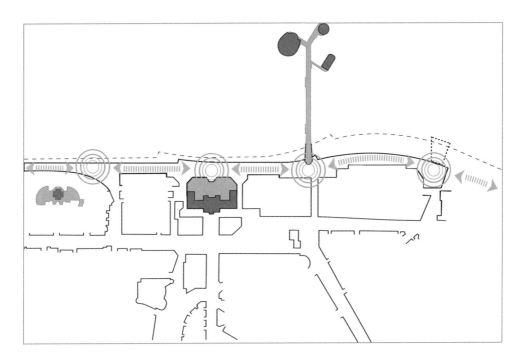

design of the boulevard connects landscape and ecology, economics and water in an attractive way that relies on coastal morphology and the history of the place.'

When asked, Voûte agrees that design can also be the enemy of the users. 'If you don't talk to the users often enough beforehand, then bad things will happen,' she says. To prevent that, the municipality is going to talk extensively with the users. 'Whereas the urban developer used to do the work because he or she understood exactly what was going on,' Voûte says, 'today we go into the city at a much earlier stage, which we call "making the city together." We gather information and we involve people in the making of plans. We consider people's ideas genuinely useful and at the same time people feel like they've been listened to. As a result, the design belongs to the people and not to the municipality.'

One of the groups that the municipality works closely with is the Beach City Foundation. Once the northern part of the boulevard in Scheveningen has been completed, then the Beach City project will be launched, which will provide the Solà Morales-boulevard with a new amenity. Beach City focuses mainly on health, sports innovation and seaside sports. The goal is make this *the* sports beach of Europe. There are representatives in the Foundation from beach and water sports, as well as owners of beach cafés and restaurants.

'You can tell that sports is becoming more and more popular, especially surfing,' Voûte says. 'Before we started to develop starting points, we asked the foundation to develop a programmatic vision. They could use it to express exactly what they needed as sportsmen and entrepreneurs, while we developed the sports beach. We incorporated many of these findings into our Beach City Developmental Plan, and now that it's our turn to tender, the foundation is one of the organisations that will evaluate the proposals.'

Of course there were bones of contention too. 'Everyone has their own interests and considerations,' Voûte explains. 'Ultimately we always ask ourselves as a municipality: is this something that will benefit the entire city? That's where the friction arises. And more generally speaking: you go to a specific spot and talk to the residents in order to find out what they want. But in the end, as a municipality, you also have to step back and ask yourself: will the rest of the city benefit from it?

Voûte and her colleagues have been working closely with developers in the northern part of the boulevard. 'We've had sessions with a developer called Sense, for example, about the area around Legoland. By the way, the market parties actually involve the residents themselves: they organise residents' evenings, to which we are also invited, though we're not asked to do anything. That, I think, is a really good development.'

DOS:

- Connect with the hinterland. The boulevard is strongly connected to what is happening in the rest of The Hague. Keep a good eye on what is really necessary.
- Visibility. The biggest drawback in the beach area around the pier in Scheveningen is that you're not sure where the sea is when you arrive. And that's not only down to the view, but also to the cobblestones and whether the wind is carrying the salty air.
- Grand gestures are fine – certainly in a coastal area – but make sure you keep things at a human level by involving people in the programming.

DON'T:

- Keep car traffic as close to the boulevard as possible. Try to intercept cars as early as possible and ensure that there are good facilities for public transport and slow traffic.

PLINTHS, PLACES AND ZEALOUS NUTS

LEARNING TO TRUST RESIDENTS AS A DRIVING FORCE

Working towards a facilitating and supportive municipality

'We don't have a Zomerhofkwartier – a climate-proof district – in Dordrecht yet; our best projects are yet to come,' says environmental psychologist and policy advisor Mariska Kien. 'Nevertheless, I think that our initial experiences of making the city a more beautiful and pleasant place together with the inhabitants is worth sharing.' As the responsible administrative person, councillor Rinette Reynvaan fully agrees.

Sometime in 2015, the subject of placemaking made it onto the agenda of the Dordrecht city council for the first time, and at the end of that year the first experiment was launched. 'The administrative agenda indicated that both Vrieseplein and Damplein were in need of maintenance,' says policy advisor Mariska Kien. 'An urban planner had even been called in already for Vrieseplein. That's when the municipality said: "No, we're going to do this differently. We're going to give residents and stakeholders a chance to determine what happens."'

'As a municipality, we really need to let go of the system that assumes we know what's best for our citizens,' adds Councillor of City Management Rinette Reynvaan, explaining why this step was taken. 'That fits the municipality's changing role, whereby the ball is in the residents' court now, and we are increasingly supportive and facilitating partner. Residents and stakeholders often come up with ideas that never would have occurred to us.'

One evening, a working group was set up consisting of people that attended an open house for Vrieseplein. Those who were not in the working group but did want contribute their ideas could approach the sounding board group. The project manager from the municipality attended the meeting, but the chair came from the working group itself.

'The way the square looks now is something that never would have occurred to the municipality,' Kien says. 'Katinka van Haren, an artist that lives on Vrieseplein, liked the idea of making a design for the pavement. After three weeks of sketching and discussing an idea materialised that was ultimately used. The residents also chose new fixtures.
The result was a creative one.'

Did things go as smoothly with Damplein?
'On Damplein, placemaking mainly ensured that a decision was finally made, after 20 years of discussions, says Kien. 'All kinds of proposals had been put forward in the past, sometimes by residents as well, but never following broad consultation. That turned out to be the only way to solve the issue, even though some things could have been done better. During the project, the working group sometimes became too involved and didn't coordinate with the district often enough. It's important that the municipality takes a position and continues to guide the process, in order to safeguard this broad consultation, for example.'

What's the most important effect of this approach?
'The city becomes more functional and appealing, and public space begins to function more effectively,' Kien explains. 'Putting the user in the spotlight means that more attention will be paid to issues that matter to residents. For example, both pilot projects put much more emphasis on the social function of the squares than had been done in the past. Furthermore, an external evaluation of people's experiences of Vrieseplein revealed that they feel much more involved in the public space when they can contribute ideas to the development. As even the chair was from the local district, residents and stakeholders had increasing confidence that they could influence decision-making processes. As a result, confidence in the board increased as well. That gave the city new energy.'

'This is happening in other places in the city as well,' says councillor Reynvaan. 'Crabbehoeve is an excellent example. An old kindergarten and playground were wasting away in one of our priority neighbourhoods. Residents asked whether they could do something with that building and land. Of course, you could come up with several objections: "Yes, but it's an old building, what's the state of the wiring? Yes, but maybe the roof will leak," and so on. We talked about that, and for the last year or two now, it is a frequently used meeting place for people in the neighbourhood. Get-togethers and meetings are held there, and residents are growing flowers and vegetables in the garden.'

What have you learned from these first two projects?
'As a municipality we really try to sit on the fence and leave as much as possible in the hands of the city,' says Kien. 'At the same time, you can't expect residents to suddenly manage a process such as placemaking – which is relatively new to us as well. I think that you need to guide the process well and have to provide clear parameters in advance. It has to be clear, for example, what the municipality can contribute financially.
We have to be much clearer about that next time: this is how much money is available, and if you want more you're going to have to find your own resources. And we can help you do that.'

'Besides, there's a City Hall here with a huge amount of expertise,' Reynvaan reiterates. 'It would be a shame not to use it. The initiative is with the residents, but we regularly meet to share plans and knowledge with each other.'

How are things going now that the project has been completed?
'Placemaking creates wonderful opportunities, but at the same time it's also a struggle sometimes for the municipality, say Kien. 'For example, there are a huge number of pigeons on Vrieseplein. They're being fed by passersby, and these creatures are pooing on everything. The residents think that the municipality should deal with that.'

'This shows how important it is to agree on expectations and opportunities in advance,' councillor Reynvaan says. 'If people put great effort into such a square, then perhaps they expect the municipality to do a major clean-up every week. That's not the case. At the same time we do need to realise: okay, it's not easy for the residents to clean up the pigeon droppings. If we agree that they clean up the litter, then we can clean the benches and pavements every now and then. Maintenance and management has to increasingly become a joint task.'

DO:

– As a municipality, sit on the fence as much as possible, but do guide the process.

DON'T:

– Identify where the energy is and don't flog a dead horse.

ACHIEVE THE IMPOSSIBLE, THAT MAKES YOU GREEDY

Schouwburgplein Rotterdam: public-private partnership 2.0

The Vereniging Verenigd Schouwburgplein ('United Theatre Square Association') so successfully redesigned and programmed the square that the municipality asked the association to take other squares under its wing as well. That's a tipping point, according to board members Bert Determann and Jeroen Laven: 'We're facing the question of how to handle a task that's too big to carry out in our current capacity.'

The Schouwburgplein in Rotterdam is one of the top-10 most beautiful squares of the world, but it's also one of the worst. Architecturally speaking, it looks fantastic viewed from above. But on the ground, the people of Rotterdam have long complained that as soon you set foot onto the square once winter has come around, you're likely to wipe out. Moreover, for years the square was notorious as a place where troublemakers gathered.

Ten years ago the municipal council asked the nine cultural partners situated on and near the square to come up with ideas about how to improve the square. 'We picked up the gauntlet and joined forces with residents, entrepreneurs and the municipality,' says Bert Determann, director of operations at the Theater Rotterdam. 'The rationale was to bring the programme from the inside to the outside and create an additional collective hall out of the square.'

Schouwburgplein Rotterdam

Flying Grass Carpet on Schouwburgplein

Modern Dance in Schouwburgplein

Today, however, Schouwburgplein is the biggest art platform situated in a square in the Netherlands. Ten years ago events were organised there 13 times a year on average. Now there are over 70 events a year. Two people were hired to handle the programming, one of whom lives on the square and can hear when there's too much noise. The other one is responsible for programming the external activities with Codarts (a university for the arts), the Film Festival, Luxor, Motel Mozaïque, Circusstad Rotterdam, to name but a few. The funding is the joint responsibility of the municipality, Rotterdam Festivals, the trade association, the cultural partners and the residents.

'Every Sunday morning, 150 people come here to do yoga,' says STIPO partner Jeroen Laven enthusiastically as he points to the square from café-restaurant Floor in the hall of the Schouwburg. Like Determann, Laven is a board member of the Vereniging Verenigd Schouwburgplein. 'The growth of activities has significantly reduced the number of complaints. The people living in the area like the events and are being well informed about them. Complaints generally arise when people aren't aware of things, and suddenly there's band playing beneath their window till midnight'

In addition to the programming, the association is also closely involved in designing the square. It has been spending time with the municipality and the designers to think about how to improve the way the square functions. This has led, among other things, to: trees being planted; making the high step to the square more accessible; and moving the ominous entrances to the car park to beneath the Pathé cinema. The number of outlets for water and electricity was also increased, so there's less mucking about with generators, and a stage was built that invites people to perform themselves. The final feat is the largest pop-up park in the world, which opened in August 2017 and will remain for at least six months. It's an initiative of Eddy Kaijser and Bart Cardinaal, who received tremendous support from the association.

'Our approach is really a pioneering one compared to other places,' Laven says. 'That's why the municipality of Rotterdam has asked us to also develop a programme for Kruisplein and Stationsplein. That's great of course, but it also means we're at a tipping point. Because how are we going to arrange all of this? The board members are all volunteers. If we're going to do this for other squares too, then we need professionals who will need to be paid. We're in a phase were we're looking for answers to the question of how to handle a task that's too big to carry out in our current capacity.'

'What we're doing here is public-private partnership 2.0,' Determann adds. 'We get involved at the administrative level with what's happening on the square, and so far our opinion has been appreciated. Once we take it a step further, then the ownership will

Feyenoord

essentially be transferred to us. In some respects that would be a good development, but it's quite a stretch. As an association, we have to address questions such as: what kind of a business model is behind this square? The interests and targets of these different squares are often miles away from each other. The Central District, for example, focuses much more on business companies and is the entrance into the city, while we're attempting to make the square much more of a place where people want to spend time. Perhaps the Central District has to incorporate more of a sense of community into its plans, whereas we should become more business-like. That's what we're looking into right now.'

The structure and composition of the association has made it possible to do things that otherwise would never have been possible. Laven cites as an example the artwork of a major waterfall that they wanted to install against a blind wall. 'Usually, that's super complicated because all of the resident associations own a piece of the wall, and of course the architect has a say in the matter too. Because everyone was represented in the association it was a piece of cake. That makes you greedy. We can't wait to do more, but the system has not been laid down yet to the extent that we can plug into it easily.'

The Schouwburgplein, for example, was the first square in the world to be included in '7 Square Endeavour', a collaborative project that aimed to prepare 7 cities across the world for a sustainable future. 'In two years,' says Laven, 'the coating of the car-park roof will need to be replaced. Of course, we want to do that in the most sustainable way in the world, and the municipality undoubtedly agrees that this is a good idea. But in the meantime, Pathé is planning to replace the façade. So if we were to tell Pathé: what a great façade, but it has to be 100% sustainable, then that won't work, because let's face it, they have their own ideas about how things should be done. We're already really happy that Pathé is willing to invest in its façade. Indeed, Pathé's branch manager sits on the association's board, but these kinds of decisions are taken by central management. The challenge is to enhance the interaction between all of these players. If you push it too much, you'll end up forcing things.'

'Sometimes our plans are premature,' Determann acknowledges, 'but sometimes you need to push them through a bit. Our golden tip, based on 10 years of placemaking experience is: start small and never lose sight of the subject matter. Save grand and spectacular for later. First prove yourself.'

DOS:

– Hang in there, even if you're knackered sometimes. Urban development means: Gradual progression.
– Make it hands-on: a joint celebration instead of bureaucracy.
– Proceed from communal initiatives and try to entice people to start programming themselves.

DON'T:

– Don't try to do things hastily, because it won't work. It can take 3 years to install a water outlet, and that's not the result of unwillingness.

THE REFRESHING WIT
OF THE HONIG COMPLEX

The housing construction along the Waal river is already in full swing, but the Honig grounds will only be needed at a much later stage. So what do you do with the complex? Demolish it or come up with a clever use? The verdict was: come up with a clever use. 'To create a good feeling in the area,' is how Henri Schimmel, development manager at BPD, explains this choice.

Schimmel views the field of area development as a search for windows of opportunity. 'When certain developments converge, you have to act vigorously. At BPD, we call it: finding and using the fordable spot.' The area around the Honing complex had a dismal air, and after the factory closed down no one went there unless necessary. BPD intended to reinvigorate the premises by giving it a temporary use. A contributing factor was the surge of interest in old industrial buildings that started to emerge just when the complex fell into disuse.

The approach used for the Honig complex is a form of placemaking, but then explicitly without a predetermined scenario. Somewhat to the surprise of BPD and the municipality the concept turned out to be a great success. For years now, the Honig complex had been bustling with energy, drawing large numbers of visitors and enjoying national fame.

In retrospect, Schimmel, who was responsible for the housing construction in the Waalfront plan, can pinpoint a few reasons for this resounding success. 'Creating something new from something old fits into today's recycling culture. Moreover, people appreciate the creative and crafts character of the Honig complex. The clustered businesses generate a lot of positive energy. And the fact that it's happening in a place where dozens of years ago industrial work was carried out from eight to five is witty and refreshing for the mind.'

So what are the ingredients for this success? Schimmel names four:

- The conditions laid down included that the start-up entrepreneurs had to be creative, pursue a craft, and fulfil a 'display window function', i.e. they had to be visible to visitors and each other.
- The temporary operations were based on a break-even result, enabling low rental prices.
- The municipality worked on and defended the chosen solution, also in relation to businesses in the inner city.
- A professional quartermaster provided guidance and supervision in selecting and providing accommodations for businesses and institutions in the Honig complex.

Hotspot with a smell of soup

For more than a century, a striking factory complex dominated the landscape just north of Nijmegen's city centre. At first it housed the corn-starch factory Hollandia, later the wheat-starch factory Latenstein, and ultimately the soup manufacturer Honig. With a westerly wind, the people of Nijmegen could enjoy the delicious bouillon aroma wafting over from the soup factory. The company was taken over in 2001 by Heinz, which stopped production in 2012 and opened an innovation centre elsewhere in the city. The high silo with the Honig logo still dominates the complex along the Waal river, which has now become a lively and popular hotspot. The 33,000 square metre complex accommodates creative and crafts businesses, including a brewery, hospitality facilities and a covered beach volleyball court. The current users can remain there until 2022. The complex is part of a new residential-business area, Waalfront, where a total of 2,100 housing units will be built until 2028. The municipality and the area developer BPD are jointly responsible for the project.

Schimmel has nothing but praise for the users, which includes brew pub Stoom and restaurant De Meesterproef. He is still immensely impressed by the way they managed to create attractive, flourishing enterprises in this huge factory complex with only simple resources. Imaginative use has been made of the uniqueness of the buildings. For example, the former lab's glass-walled rooms, arranged around a central hall, were converted into workshops by culinary entrepreneurs.

The Honig complex is nearly self-supporting. The quartermaster has been replaced by a manager who also resides in the complex. The municipality and BPD only take care of the finances or come to the rescue when calamities occur, such as a major leakages.

The big question is: how to proceed from here? Initially, the Honig complex was to be demolished after 2022 to make room for residential housing. But even many die-hard sceptics are now embracing the complex like a favourite son. Politicians who have been advocating demolition are now encountering resistance. Schimmel

shakes his head when talking about it. He observes a lot of t=0 – or short-term thinking. 'The magic of the place is largely determined by its temporary nature and fresh energy,' he says. 'But this will be different in ten years' time. Then you'll have to deal, more than now, with a discontent inner city and the need for investment.'

On the other hand, he also realises that the temporary occupation plan has exceeded expectations. That's why he can understand today's mindset. 'We asked BOEi, who focus on the restoration and reallocation of cultural heritage sites, to analyse the complex. The analysis revealed that many industrial buildings are not worth saving, but the brick buildings that form the core of the complex are perhaps saveable.' Today's mindset tends towards preserving some of the buildings and making them suitable for living, working and various facilities. Moreover, the idea is to retain something of the Honig atmosphere – described by Schimmel as a 'rambling industrial area' – and incorporate it into the urban development plan for the new housing estates, Handelskade and Koningsdaal, situated nearby.

The Honig complex and the procedures involved proved enlightening to BPD. 'I learned that it's worth the effort to allow for spontaneity and flexibility in the development of the plan,' says Schimmel. 'Although you must maintain strict control and never lose sight of your goal. The flexibility mainly applies to the process.'

In retrospect he thinks he might have done things differently. 'More thought should have been given to the question: What will we do if the project becomes a big success? Now it has overwhelmed us all a bit. Perhaps we should have anticipated that Honig was a fordable spot and capitalised on it more for Waalfront's area branding.'

Schimmel expects that the Honig case will definitely influence the way BPD operates in the future. 'We're traditionally involved more in expansion than in infill development. These ratios are now reversed. Honig is a great test case in this respect. Although you can't use the same approach everywhere, and not every factory complex is suitable for conversion.'

By switching to urban construction, BPD is increasingly transforming into an area brander who has to try to merge both existing and future functions. But an area brander is different than a placemaker, emphasises Schimmel. 'Placemaking means enabling the Honig complex to function well. Area branding applies to the larger context, to the Waalfront programme, and covers a longer time frame.'

Placemaking, however, is an important advantage in area branding, he explains. 'The way placemaking took place with the Honig complex has a value-enhancing effect. It's no coincidence that the Honig cargo bike graces the brochures for the Koningsdaal quarter. Housing prices in Waalfront are considerably higher than in Waalsprong, on the opposite side of the river. Honig has functioned as a multiplier in the area's branding.'

DO:

– Focus continuously on the area development's joint goals and have the guts to achieve these goals, while understanding and respecting the interests and roles of the parties involved.

DON'T:

– Avoid focusing on short-term interests and allow for spontaneity and flexibility in the planning process.

JOINT VISION OF A BEACH ON THE ZAAN

As we stroll along the south-eastern side of the Zaan river through Zaanstad on this warm July day, we can already see Simone Ronchetti and Laura Dumas sitting on a bench in the distance. They're active members of the community-based initiative 'Tussen Zuiddijk en Zaan', which is trying to enhance this area's quality of living. Simone has a folder with her containing everything that has been achieved in three years. But even without the folder, some of the results are clearly visible: the benches and flowerboxes on the quay weren't there a few years ago. And the charming signpost that indicates what there is to do in the neighbourhood was the community group's initiative. Yet satisfaction is not the predominating sentiment among these two women. 'You can see that a lot has happened here, but I wouldn't go as far as to say: what a great place to be…' Ronchetti kicks off the discussion.

But first, back to how it all began. When Fred Kent and Kathy Madden were in the Netherlands in 2014, one of the places they visited was the area between Zuiddijk and Zaan. De Burcht, a large square used for parking and events, is situated right in the middle of this area. On the east side is Zuiddijk, a well-known shopping street that was in need of a bit of livening up. To the west is the Zaan river, which has a quay where cruise ships sometimes dock. The area in between consists of residential streets.

The neighbourhood is situated right opposite the centre of Zaanstad. This part of the city has looked a bit forlorn according to its residents, especially since the city centre was given a major makeover. On the other side of the water there are two beautiful new benches, for example, whereas the benches on the quay are hand-me-downs from other neighbourhood. 'And they clean everyday there, but not here,' says Ronchetti despondently. 'At first it was even worse here though,' Dumas recalls. 'Before the flowerboxes and benches appeared, there where high concrete walls along the quay. It looked like a small neglected room.'

The visit of Kent and Madden stirred things up, both at the municipality and among residents. 'We from the real world wanted to shake up the system a little. Get the neighbourhood to take action by getting its people to set their own agenda and come up with proposals,' says Saskia de Man, strategic advisor of social affairs for the municipality, who took on this challenge together with neighbourhood manager Laura van Nooij. 'It made me look at my neighbourhood differently,' says resident Laura Dumas. 'The final report of the Placemaking Game mentioned things like a beach on the Zaan', Simone Ronchetti recalls.

One of the outcomes of the visit was the establishment of the shopping street association Tussen Zuiddijk en Zaan. Its aim was to promote quality of life in the neighbourhood through a partnership consisting of residents and entrepreneurs. The association started expeditiously. It hung historical photos of the neighbourhood behind the windows of the vacant Aldi supermarket. The association provided the neighbourhood with Chinese lanterns for the Dam to Dam road running race. It also organised a winter party and a spring market. A life-size chess board and temporary outdoor cinema appeared in De Burcht. The association managed to get a small grant for the neighbourhood signpost during the 'Stad aan de the Zaan' event. Mothers mobilised children to join a cleaning team, and InstaWalks were organised.

The importance of small initiatives

In June 2014, a placemaking process began in Zaanstad. Fred Kent and Kathy Madden from the Project for Public Spaces from the United States paid the city a visit at the time and supervised a placegame. About 30 residents, entrepreneurs and public servants participated. They assessed the practical value of five locations on the west and on the east side of the Zaan river. They formulated quick wins and actions that need to be taken for each location in the mid to long term, and considered who could take the initiative. Inspired by this, the community group 'Tussen Zuiddijk en Zaan' undertook a series of community-based initiatives. Other initiatives in Zaanstad involving placemaking include 'Aan de Zaan', a network platform and podium for social and cultural initiatives to make Zaandstad more beautiful and more fun, and LAB.z, a public place and intermediary where residents, entrepreneurs and the municipality can experiment together, share knowledge and search together for creative and practical solutions for urban issues.

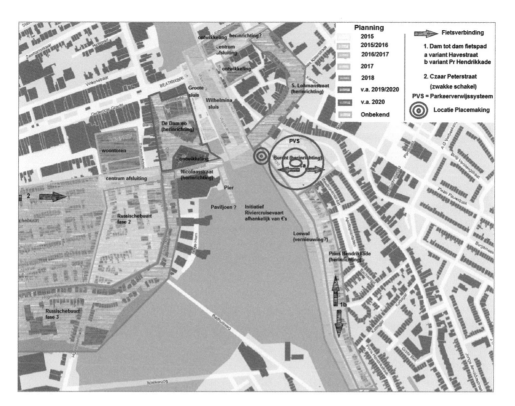

Planning

2015
2015/2016
2016/2017
2017
2018
v.a. 2019/2020
v.a. 2020
Onbekend

Fietsverbinding

1. Dam tot dam fietspad
a variant Havestraat
b variant Pr Hendrikkade

2. Czaar Peterstraat
(zwakke schakel)

PVS = Parkeerverwijssysteem

Locatie Placemaking

A great deal is happening in collaboration with the municipality. Area manager Coos Hoekstra, who has since retired, procured the benches and flowerboxes. He was often present in the area, trying to get his colleagues in the city hall to hit the streets too, and residents could always approach him with questions and requests. Yet the partnership with the municipality has not always been as smooth as it could be. Ronchetti cites the example of the waste bins. Benches need waste bins. The municipality only placed one there. It overflowed, which caused a nuisance. So the association asked for more waste bins. 'We were given two more. But on condition that we would empty them ourselves. Luckily the municipal caretaker empties our bins sometimes too. But something like just makes your heart sink into your boots.'

The partnership with the shopkeepers on Zuiddijk is more strained. They have their own association and seem to view the new initiative more as a rival than a companion. The retailers, with the exception of café De Schot, are working against most of the neighbourhood initiatives instead of embracing them. In the meantime, the shopping street association has renamed itself a neighbourhood association. These kinds of setbacks has dampened the enthusiasm among residents, though they do appreciate the activities organised by the association.

In the meantime, the Maak.Zaanstad programme was introduced. At the city level, it actually has the same aim as Tussen Zuiddijk en Zaan: make a joint investment in the quality of life in society. Initially, the new programme appeared to be particularly unfavourable for the neighbourhood: the redevelopment of De Burcht was postponed in anticipation of the outcomes of Maak.Zaanstad. But Ronchetti does see some light at the end of the tunnel. 'Until now, this was the attitude: come what may, in the end it's the municipality that decides. I'm hoping that Maak.Zaanstad will change things.' Dumas adds that 'we are now seen as a partner and taken seriously, so that makes a difference.' 'That's true, Ronchetti says, we're regularly invited to participate in discussions now.'

Experiences such as the one with Tussen Zuiddijk en Zaan have been making all kinds of things happen at the municipal level too. Public servants have become more aware of the value of placemaking and what resident groups have to offer. 'We want to use the lessons learned with De Burcht to ensure that Maak. Zaanstad is a success,' Saskia de Man says. 'I'm thinking of effective agenda-setting, resident input and literally trying to bring in future investments.'

Meanwhile the residents still have ambitious dreams: from major developments à la Paris Plages, the artificial beaches that the municipality of Paris create every summer along the Seine, to initiatives such as Amsterdam's WeTheCity and De Ceuvel. They have remained realistic, however, as a result of the setbacks and realise that improving your neighbourhood takes place step by step. 'Maybe we should paint the shed of the quayside electricity facility one day,' says Dumas, pointing towards a small stone building on the quay from her bench on the Zaan. 'Yes, then at least people will notice that something's happening,' Ronchetti agrees.

Coos Hoekstra reiterates the importance of this. 'Major programmes such as Maak. Zaanstad are good but are quick to get in the way of placemaking. And residents are eager to continue as long the energy is still there. So it's important to ensure that small things keep happening during long-term projects.'

DO:

– As a resident, approach all parties, forge partnerships with public servants and use them to your advantage. As a public servant, approach citizens, hit the streets. For all parties: make sure you're open-minded. And have consideration for each other, the space and time.

DON'T:

– Some things don't work, but never give up hope.

THE BELFORT SQUARE: FROM A BLEAK SQUARE TO A BOOMING RESTAURANT HUB

Almere Centre had started to deteriorate shortly before the onset of the economic crisis. Entrepreneurs, owners and the municipality realised that something had to change, so they joined forces. The crowded outdoor cafés on the previously deserted Belfort Square are a testament to the success of their approach.

'In 2006, shortly before the outbreak of the crisis, a huge area was added to our centre,' explains Danny Louwerse, programme manager of the Almere municipality. He points to the 'new build' on the spacious square in front of City Hall, where it was already pretty lively for a Tuesday morning. 'Many retailers moved to the "new build", which in the years that followed created an enormous vacancy rate in the old part of the centre. The remaining retailers rebelled and the situation escalated increasingly.'

It was evident that something had to happen. In 2011/2012 the Centre Partners (see box) hired the creative consultancy agency Fresh Forward and the Next Level trajectory was started. They came up with the plaza strategy: a vision for

The Centre Partners

The successful placemaking project in Almere Centre is, first and foremost, the result of a close collaboration between the parties involved. The new Belfortplein (Belfort Square) has been initiated and realised by:
- Unibail Rodamco
- Ondernemersvereniging Stadscentrum Almere (OVSA) [Almere City Centre Trade Association]
- Almere City Marketing (ACM)
- Platform Almere Centre (PAC) [residents' platform]
- Municipality of Almere

this area, in which placemaking was central and where every square had its own identity. The common theme was: there is always something exciting going on in Almere, the eternally young city.

An editorial board was subsequently established in which all important parties were represented: the major property owners, the trade association, the residents, the colleges, Almere City Marketing and the cultural institutions. Together they explored the options. What do we have? How can we give shape to the plaza strategy?

'Starting in 2013, the Centre Partners began to 'practice' on Belfort Square,' says programme secretary Marijke Kuijpers. 'When you walked across Belfort Square in those days, you thought: "Help, I'm lost" and you wanted to get away as quickly as possible. It was just outside the centre; there was a hairdresser, a fishmonger and a small shop from the municipality. That was it! Belfort was a bleak and empty square nobody wanted to go to.'

That is hard to imagine today. Children whiz down the slides next to the stairs that provide access to the square. The restaurants and other hospitality establishments that are now located in nearly all of the premises have awnings in soft hues, and colourful planters form the separations between the outdoor cafés. The identity assigned to Belfort Square in the plaza strategy concept can be summed up as 'indulgence': 'It's simply crowded every night.'

The reason for commencing with the implementation of the plaza strategy on Belfort Square was that Unibail-Rodamco, which owned all of the premises there, came with an initial proposal to transform the square into a hospitality plaza.

However, that meant that the businesses established there had to move. 'They were very understanding,' says Louwerse. 'Everyone knew: we can't continue that way; nobody was making a living anymore. So when the editorial board asked whether they supported their relocation, they replied that they didn't really want to leave now that things were getting better, but that they understood.'

Apart from these relocations, the outside space underwent a redevelopment and all entrepreneurs worked jointly on the programme. A kiosk in the middle of the square, which had been vacant for ages because the owners couldn't make a go of it, was demolished. Unibail invested in the awnings that give the square a Mediterranean flair, and the new businesses made a one-time investment in the public space. Louwerse: 'A case in point is the slide and the trampoline near the stairs. Together with the editorial board we decided that if we want to be an eternally young city, we have to provide a place for children where they can have fun while their parents are sitting in the outdoor café. And that's when we came up with great features such as the trampoline and slide.'

Desire Path

The first steps on the way to the transformation of the next two squares will have to be initiated before the end of 2017: the Esplanade and Stationsplein (Station Square). But first, Louwerse and Kuijpers want to experiment a great deal more with placemaking by organising small-scale events with the city. A case in point is a mini beach that will emerge shortly on the Esplanade and where student associations can hold beach volleyball tournaments. Louwerse: 'We want to involve the city as much as possible. Otherwise you may end up with a beautiful square that no one uses... We don't want that to happen. That's why I often walk around the Esplanade in the early morning to observe where it is dirty. Because that means people have sat there and those are the spots we have to focus on strongly. In my earlier days at urban regeneration I witnessed that a former desire path was blocked off with a fence. It would have made more sense to build a walkway there, because that's where people use the city.'

The colourful stickers on the windows effectively distract attention from the few buildings in the plaza that are still unoccupied. In order to optimally facilitate placemaking, the department *Vergunningverlening Toezicht en Handhaving* (Licensing, Supervision and Enforcement) is currently working on transferring the responsibility for outdoor café licensing to Unibail so that they can plan the outdoor cafés without hindrance. Louwerse: 'We are shifting the responsibilities increasingly towards the owner. Why not? They invest millions in this space and they want to recoup their investments, so they don't take measures unless they believe they'll be successful. Moreover, the tenants only have to deal with one party – it works better that way.'

Louwerse did not venture to predict whether this would ultimately lead to the full privatisation of the public space. 'We keep taking small steps in this direction. The clean-up of the space, for example, is partly already in the hands of the property owners.'

Monitoring research revealed that the Belfort Square's appeal has increased tremendously. Its current image is that of a vibrant square

where there's always something to do. This is attributable not only
to the redevelopment but certainly also the placemaking efforts. For
instance, Unibail has concluded an agreement with the entrepreneurs
that entails experimenting with a variety of activities. One of the events
is a monthly cooking workshop given by a well-known chef. In addition,
there is an annual Outdoor Café Festival that runs through the entire city,
culminating at Belfort Square in all sorts of samplings and tastings, as
well as live music. Louwerse: 'The idea came up when we had podiums
set up that weren't used between King's Day and Liberation Day
on 5 May. What a waste.'

Another example are the urban gardens. Grass mats were rolled out
throughout the entire shopping centre and rented out to residents and
entrepreneurs, on which they could sell sustainable products. Kuijpers:
'The idea for this festival came from the editorial board and the Trade
Association took the lead in the implementation. In fact, the municipality
only issued the licences. It's amazing: people queue up to secure
such a mini garden!'

Three years after the commencement of the transformation, the only
minor problem remaining on Belfort Square is the mosaic-embellished
clock: 'Belfort needs a clock, but this mosaic clock has already been
moved once before and now it's in the way again because there is a
need for more outdoor cafés.'

DOS:

- Work together closely with all parties involved (and take all of them
  seriously)
- Keep interaction with the city going
- Try out what works and what doesn't

DON'TS:

- Do more than just talk
- Don't start redeveloping without first analysing current use
- Don't lose track of the big picture

HARVESTING THE INCENTIVE FOR A GREAT ZOHO AT EYE LEVEL

ZOHO, as Zomerhofkwartier is often referred to, is an industrial estate just a ten-minute walk from Rotterdam Central Station. For years it was a no-go area. Vacant business properties, rundown streets and closed façades didn't make the area particularly inviting. Anyone walking down Zomerhofstraat today can drink a café latte or a Noordtsingle beer at a trendy outdoor café. Now the area is attracting an increasing number of people. Since 2013, the housing association Havensteder, the municipality and entrepreneurs have joined forces to literally break open the area. An incentive grant of 100,000 euros provided by the municipality to address the plinths and outside area (the city at eye level) was an excellent opportunity to kick things off.

What's special about the project?
'We applied for the grant as a consortium,' says Paul Elleswijk, project leader at Havensteder, 'together with the municipality and with entrepreneurs from all over Zomerhofkwartier.' Maria Kluijtenaar, trainee in housing policy at Havensteder explains: 'When applying for financing you usually have to meet all kinds of requirements. But everything was very open with this project.' Jacco Bakker, area manager for the north of Rotterdam, adds: 'We included the investment from entrepreneurs in our proposal. Twenty entrepreneurs will each dedicate 100 hours to the project. This commitment has also enabled us to expand our network. The project shows what the social returns are and how you can encourage others to invest as well.' 'Not everyone at the municipality was in favour of awarding an incentive grant to an area where few people were investing in financially, but the project was approved,' Paul says. 'The Urban Development

Department often backs larger systematic interventions,' Jacco says.
'This project's approach was far more process-driven and intricate.
Not everyone has a feel for that, and as a result fewer of these kinds of
projects come their way. So it's special that the municipality decided to
take on this experiment in the end.'

How did you involve other parties?
'When the money was granted,' Jacco says, 'the big question was how to
further develop the project without shutting out possibilities.' 'We didn't
want to make the mistake of doing everything ourselves,' Paul says. 'We
involved STIPO and together we organised a placegame and asked our
partners to submit and present their plans. That created a lot of energy.
It was also an opportunity to draw attention to the overall area and get
people from different buildings to work together. Havensteder also
contributed another 25,000 euros.'

'We then set up a jury,' says Paul, 'with three partners: Havensteder,
STIPO and the municipality. The three of us quickly agreed on allocation,
but it was trickier to show that our assessment was objective and
transparent. In the end, there were eight proposals, all of which were
honoured. Every initiative was worthwhile. Some initiatives received the
entire amount that they applied for whereas other received a portion of
that amount. For the latter group, we tried to figure out what kinds of other
support would help their projects move forward.'

The accepted projects include the frontage for Broeinest on Zomerhofstraat, now completed, a frontage for 'de Mafkees' ('Nutcase') Hostel, which is in the pipeline, a project that wants to make better use of sidewalks and make them more lively by installing benches and flowerpots, and refurbishing the entrance to Marché 010, a new market hall. There are also art projects, such as the application of illuminated letters and a project with light boxes/open windows. These are all interventions in the plinth in the broadest sense of the term.

What has been achieved one year after awarding the proposals?
'The plan was to complete all of the projects within a year,' says Paul. 'Only one of the projects has been implemented after a year, while four projects are due to be completed soon, one has been cancelled and two are uncertain. In practice, realising projects can be quite complicated. I am disappointed by that.' 'I'm not so disappointed,' Jacco says, 'but I had hoped for things to go smoother. But it takes time. That's an inherent aspect of trying to do a great deal with little money. Each of the eight projects is being carried out by the applicants themselves. That's a considerable responsibility: you're being asked to handle every aspect of the project, from A to Z. These people also have to deal with matters that they normally aren't confronted with and know little about. The application for a building permit turned out to be an obstacle for a young entrepreneur, for example. We weren't sufficiently aware of these things beforehand.' Maria adds: 'For many entrepreneurs a project like this means extra work. They do it on the side. That's not the case for entrepreneurs whose own business is directly affected by the project. Building the frontage of Broeinest was directly linked to the business and to an establishment criterion to occupy the building.'

How do you view your own roles?
'I think that we could be more visible,' Maria says. 'There's no clear contact person at the municipality or Havensteder, and it's not always clear where the responsibility lies. People also want to be sure that they can get to work and won't be pulled back by the municipality or the owner of the building.' 'We could communicate better about the approach,' Jacco says, 'spending time on showcasing our success stories and referring people on more often. Communication is a bit of a neglected child.'

'Social capital is not one of Havensteder's strong points,' Paul says. 'Social return is hard to measure, and therefore it's difficult to get internal support for it. You're always confronted with construction setbacks in these kinds of buildings. That's another hurdle in the process that needs to be overcome.' 'There's not always understanding at the municipality either,' Jacco says. 'It's kind of viewed as straying from the beaten path. But so much has changed in the area: the liveliness, the atmosphere, the use of Zomerhofstraat. The fence around Scrap and the door of Marché 010 have become much more attractive. The project also gave us a clear reason to continue to meet with the other partners in the area and exchange ideas.' 'I hope,' Paul says, 'that later we'll be able to show that the positive developments in recent years are still going strong.' 'The incentive grant enables you to produce quality, and that raises the bar for future partners who want to invest in ZOHO,' Jacco says.

DOS:

– Work with as many stakeholders as possible from the area. As a municipality, you can challenge partners and give them the freedom to come up with something. That makes it possible to get a development started or support one with relatively little money.
– Further develop the project at the organisational level. Earmark funds for man hours for supervision. That will save you a great deal of time and energy.

DON'TS:

– Forget to think carefully in advance about ownership and responsibilities.
– Give too much freedom, provide no guidelines whatsoever or, conversely, shut out all possibilities. Try to strike a balance in these matters.

SLEEPING BENEATH MORE THAN FOUR STARS

Open-Air Hotel Van Schaffelaar

Hotel Van Schaffelaar is the first real open-air hotel in the Netherlands. The hotel is a performative intervention in public space in which the active participation of the public is indispensable. The participation is what makes the performance, which begins right after the guest checks in and a host takes you to your bed.

The programme takes you through the night and the morning. It includes an open-air cinema related to the theme of freedom and a wellness area with a hot tub, as well as singer-songwriters at the foot of your bed and storytellers that whisper a story into your ear before going to bed.

At sunrise – as the guests slowly wake up outdoors – local residents serve breakfast. After the guests check out around eleven o'clock, the hotel is dismantled. Two hours later, there's not a single trace of it anymore.

DON'T TAKE FREEDOM FOR GRANTED

The idea for an open-air hotel came about during a collaboration between artists from Cascoland and placemakers from Urbanboost, two parties that are actively involved in a neighbourhood called Kolenkitbuurt in Amsterdam. In the context of 4 and 5 May – the commemoration of German occupation and the celebration of freedom – they wanted to make a statement.

Staying at the open-air hotel is a unique sleep experience, but even more important than that are the people that the guests meet and the stories that they exchange. While many of us take our freedom for granted, that isn't the case for people who have had to flee from unsafe areas or have family and friends abroad who still live in unsafe conditions every day.

Kolenkitbuurt is one of the most multicultural neighbourhoods in Amsterdam, with a great deal of variation when it comes to background, income and education. In recent years, there has been an influx of refugees and holders of residence permits: all of these residents have their own story and experiences to tell and their own notion of safety and freedom.

THE PROJECT DEVELOPERS BEHIND THE HOTEL

In 2015, Cascoland already had an actor sleep overnight on Jan van Schaffelaarplantsoen in Kolenkitbuurt for its promotional event 'Hé Gast' ('Hey guest/dude': 'gast' means both guest and dude in Dutch, ed.) to show that the alleged safety problem in the neighbourhood wasn't so bad after all. Which was true: instead of bothering the sleeping guest, the young locals took him under their wing.

Cascoland believes that 'putting yourself in a vulnerable position' provides more assurances of social safety in public space than if you were to design and programme it with vandalism in mind. An example of this is a glass house as a community meeting place in public space, as is cycling together in conflict areas, such as Palestine or a South African township, or sleeping in public space in the 'worst neighbourhood in the Netherlands'.

Urbanboost focuses on local communities, based on the notion that users know best what's really needed to improve the quality of life in their environment. Previously, it organised freedom meals with the successful community initiative Boloboost – founded to give a positive boost to the deprived area of Bos en Lommer (BoLo). Local residents prepared meals at other residents' houses and then served the food in a park to 250 other neighbourhood residents.

Sleeping outside in public space and serving freedom meals both concern feeling safe in your own environment. These kinds of initiatives make people conscious of the fact that not everyone shares the freedom that we take for granted. Cascoland and Urbanboost wanted to spread this message to a wider audience. The idea for the open-air Hotel Van Schaffelaar came about after a bit of brainstorming ('what if we put forty beds in public space one day and offered the guests a stay over in the open air?').

BUSINESS RISK

In order to ensure some commitment from guests and to keep tabs on the hotel's occupancy, guests could book beds online with Cascoland – the latter because many people in Kolenkit are not so skilled at using the internet. Thanks to promotion via social and local media, both hotels were completely booked in no time (2016 and 2017). There were as many people interested from the neighbourhood as there were from other parts of the city.
They were all curious about this unique sleeping experience.
The returns from the ticket sales (€10 per bed, including breakfast), the contributions from the municipality, the sponsors and the many volunteers made it possible for the 'one-night hotel' to break even.

Something else that needs to be taken into consideration is that when an individual wants to sleep in the open air, that's fine. But when forty people want to sleep outside simultaneously, even if that takes place in public space, you need a license. The latter was issued without any questions asked, by the way.

Another important aspect of sleeping beneath the stars is the weather. The nights can still be quite cold in early May. That's why the guests were asked to bring appropriate warm clothing and sleeping bags.

Having people sleep in the open air means that you have to have a contingency plan for when things don't go as planned. If rain showers were forecasted, then the hotel was cancelled. If there was a small chance of rain, then there was a sheltered alternative. But there wasn't much chance that permission would be granted for that. That's why a licence was never requested and the location was never announced. Luckily the weather gods were in a good mood on both occasions.

In the meantime, there's a spin-off: the Open-Air Community Garden. The first online reviews show how popular this 'one-night hotel' concept is already:

'It was so beautiful in the hotel! Thanks to all of the staff for a great stay (and for tucking us in so lovingly! ☺)' – Annemarie

'This was beyond great! Thanks so much ☺ I forgot my swimming gear, though. You didn't find it by any chance, did you?' – Nicole

THE FLYING GRASS CARPET, THE TRAVELLING CITY PARK

The Flying Grass Carpet travels around the world, just like in fairy tales. It travels from city to city, and from square to square. This artwork acts like a welcoming city park. Picnics are held spontaneously, frisbees fly through the air in the middle of the city and children are happily racing around because this is where gym class is being held now.

The Flying Grass Carpet looks like a gigantic Persian rug and is made of different kinds and colours of artificial grass. Whenever The Flying Grass Carpet comes to a city, people greet it enthusiastically. It creates spontaneous encounters and bonds citizens. Two Rotterdam agencies are responsible for the concept, design and execution: HUNK-design and Studio ID Eddy.

INVITING PUBLIC SPACES

The concept for The Flying Grass Carpet was developed in 2007. It began with two objectives: improve public spaces in cities and create a bond between people living in cities around the world. Since an increasing number of people choose to live in cities there is a growing demand for attractive public spaces. The Flying Grass Carpet is capitalising on this need.

A family of Carpets has been developed that will turn any location into a positive experience: The Flying Grass Carpet Original, The Junior Carpet and The Baby Carpet. The sizes of the Carpets vary from 45 to 900 square metres. All of them are made of colourful artificial grass.

Plinths, Places and Zealous Nuts

The appearance, inspired by Persian rugs, instantly creates a soft, inviting and homely atmosphere in all of these squares. That's evident from their use. The Willy-Brand-Platz in Essen, which locals used to cross and never linger, was transformed into a square that was a popular venue for birthday parties. The Grotekerkplein in Rotterdam was suddenly discovered by bootcampers who started to train there. And in the evening, Madrileno friends met at the stony courtyard of the Matadero to enjoy the cool evening air. The Flying Grass Carpets travelled to more than 20 destinations: from nearby Rotterdam to faraway China.

THE GIANT

The family of Carpets was expanded in August 2017 with The Giant. This new Carpet was designed specially for the Rotterdam Schouwburgplein. The Carpet covers a surface area of 3,500 square metres, which makes it the largest Carpet in the series and even the biggest pop-up park in the world. The Giant is composed of smaller carpets, intended to give the scale of the square more human proportions. Every individual Carpet contains an architectural Rotterdam icon that has been worked into a floral pattern. Large, living plants have been added to the pop-up park to further enhance the perception of green. It's important to mention that the Schouwburgplein ranks eighth on a list compiled by Project for Public Spaces (PPS) identifying squares in the world most urgently in need of improvement. This pop-up park serves as inspirer and test case for future adaptations of the square.

PLACETESTING

Studio ID Eddy and HUNK-design initiated their own method of placemaking with the design of The Flying Grass Carpet. When you regularly walk past a place or spend time in it, then you no longer notice certain characteristics. As a result, you lose track of the location's potential. What the designers of The Flying Grass Carpet have managed to do is to get people to temporarily perceive the spot in a different light. People slow down, sit on the Carpet and literally look at this familiar place from a different perspective.

By injecting more quality into a square, The Flying Grass Carpet provides new inspiration and heightened ambition. The designers call this placetesting. The Flying Grass Carpet has been deployed in a targeted way in several cities to gain experience that can be applied in new designs for squares. This concept was recognised in 2009 with a Dutch Design Award, and in 2014 it earned a place on The CNN 10: Better by Design list.

ADVENTURES

Another aspect of The Flying Grass Carpet is that it gives city dwellers around the globe a sense of community. When you sit on the Carpet and your fingers touch the grass, you can imagine someone in Shenzhen or Berlin having done exactly the same thing. You see a child jump from colour block to colour block and you know that there were kids playing just like that in Pécs. The main insight gained from ten years of experience with The Flying Grass Carpet is that people all over the world respond identically to an inviting public space. They share the same curiosity, playful attitude and need for relaxation, wherever they are.

TIPS AND TRICKS

The travels of The Flying Grass Carpet have demonstrated that it's important to give public spaces a touch of softness and colour. That you need to break up large empty spaces and render them on a more human scale. Experiment with playful interventions, for children as well as adults. And most important of all: design a public space that's appealing and inviting

The Flying Grass Carpet will embark on many more beautiful journeys in the future, create a bond between city residents and continue to inspire. You can follow its adventures on www.flyinggrasscarpet.org.

If you're dreaming of The Flying Grass Carpet paying a visit to your city, then contact Bart Cardinaal, Nadine Roos (HUNK-design) or Eddy Kaijser (Studio ID Eddy). Who knows, maybe your town or city will become part of The Flying Grass Carpet's adventurous fairy tale journeys.

'BAKING BREAD FOR LASTING CHANGE'

'If I ever have trouble making ends meet, I'm going to become a baker,' artist and social designer Peik Suyling always said. As an artist in the cultural sector, he had trouble making ends meet during the financial crisis. That's what led him to start a bakery. He soon noticed that it was drawing people. The loss of work, money and security had created a need in people to share stories, experiences and solutions. And that's how Bakery De Eenvoud ('Simplicity') came to see the light of day, a mobile bakery that serves as a place to 'look for simplicity in complex issues'.

'Bread symbolises simplicity because it consists merely of water, flour, yeast and salt, and it's easy to make; it's a simple process but shouldn't be underestimated.' That's how Sander van der Ham explains the name and nature of the project. Van der Ham, affiliated to STIPO as an urban psychologist, was involved in De Eenvoud from the start. 'We developed the concept together. Peik acted as baker and I was his helper, he says jokingly. 'Actually that suited me, because I like to observe. We go to exciting places, such as disadvantaged and shrinking neighbourhoods. These are places dealing with extremely complex issues, such as providing care for each other where that is not a given or places where public servants are unable to reach people. We just show up and then see what happens.'

Bakery De Eenvoud consists of a blue construction trailer with a wood-fired clay oven. It can be towed by car to any desired location. The very first Bakery De Eenvoud was set up in Amsterdam. After that our bakeries appeared in a village in Groningen called Hongerige Wolf ('Hungry Wolf') and on the island of Vlieland. But Bakery De Eenvoud goes to many places, such as Wijk aan Zee, Rotterdam, Amersfoort, Amsterdam and Schiedam. The shelter with the oven is always placed in a public location. Piek and Sander go around the neighbourhood and hand out flyers and posters to notify residents.

'The best is when you arrive somewhere early, as is fitting for a baker,' Van der Ham says with a sparkle in his eyes. 'The wood-fired clay oven is shaped like a dome. You have to fire it for more than two hours before it reaches the right temperature. In the meantime, you open the door and people can come inside. No, we don't have any lettering. We do put a chalkboard outside though. And of course people see the chimney on the roof and smell the burning wood and later the bread.'

Once the trailer is there, everyone's welcome. 'We try to create a good atmosphere. People can help us or just have a look around or have a chat. Everything's allowed, no one is obliged to do anything,' according to Van der Ham. In the Groningen hamlet Hongerige Wolf, he and Suyling were already out and about at five in the morning. By nine o'clock there still wasn't a single visitor in sight. 'But at ten after nine the place was full,' says Van der Ham, smiling. 'Almost the entire village came by. It's a village with seventy houses, but it turned out there were people there who didn't know, after twenty years, what their neighbour did. Imagine what that's like in the city.'

The reason for descending on Hongerige Wolf at the north-eastern tip of Groningen was that it's situated in a shrinking region. 'But that subject didn't appeal to these people at all. "Shrinking?" That's not happening at all,' they said. What did concern them, though, was what it would be like to become old there. Will we be lonelier if there are fewer services? There were animated discussions about that. And it ultimately meant that the village had its own bakery: a meeting place for residents.'

The visitors' behaviour differed considerably. 'Older white men in particular initially sat there passively, with their arms crossed. Moroccan women, on other hand, took everything off your hands immediately. Sometimes they say that they recognise the clay oven from Morocco, where people always chatted with each other. A lot of them still bake their own bread.'

Usually, the atmosphere gradually opens up and more people get involved in the conversation. Those who help out automatically meet strangers while kneading the dough or waiting for the bread to rise and bake. Often, the conversations are about the neighbourhood and the needs and wishes of those present.

Why does De Eenvoud work so well? 'It's a completely different approach than having a public servant go to a neighbourhood and ask people what their concerns are,' says Van der Ham. 'In such cases, their approach is: we have a problem, what are we going to do about it? That often makes people go into denial. Or they become preoccupied about a problem that's hardly there. People are relaxed while baking bread. Kneading the dough in particular takes them out of their comfort zone and results in conversations that are different than their usual ones. They talk about what they can do together, how they can shape their future.'

Sometimes there's a theme. For example, De Eenvoud headed for the heart of Amsterdam in 2016 on the Dag van de Mantelzorg ('Day of Caregiving'). The municipality had looked into it and found that 20% of the 7,000 caregivers in the city centre were overworked, but that only 6% were asking for help. 'The professionals said: they simply don't approach us. But more than 150 people came to us that day, including overworked caregivers. We put some of them in touch with welfare institutions. We worked with a caregiving centre called Markant. After that, a meeting was held one evening where ideas were thrown into the group, such as a 24-hour helpline. It shows that you can expand your network simply by going to a neighbourhood.'

As temporary as De Eenvoud's stays always are, they regularly generate lasting change. That happened on Vlieland, where there was a mobile oven that was placed on a variety of locations on the island by the forestry commission. In Amersfoort, an ancient oven from an old courtyard with almshouses was restored to reinstate the tradition of baking bread for the neighbourhood. And in Hongerige Wolf, the residents built an oven made of Groningen clay, which was donated by a brick factory, and placed it in a mobile shed. They regularly hold baking events on Sundays, and they also fire the oven during their annual festival. Just like De Eenvoud, they journey into the wide world, though they limit themselves to the surrounding villages because they move their shed by tractor.

A social form of placemaking, that's what Van der Ham calls Bakery De Eenvoud. And one that's easy to set up. Because De Eenvoud doesn't have to comply with building or environmental regulations. Indeed, Van der Ham highly recommends it to municipal administrations and welfare institutions. 'Just go with Bakery De Eenvoud and stand in a neighbourhood for a few hours a month to bake bread, things are guaranteed to happen. It's similar to organising a placegame, you make new connections, which creates a foundation that the neighbourhood's residents can build on to achieve lasting change. The strength of the bakery is that it's an easy way to link up formal parties and informal networks in neighbourhoods and villages that you can connect to each other.'

WETHECITY: FROM BOILING EVENTS TO THE WORLD'S BIGGEST OPEN-AIR CAFÉ

WeTheCity improves the human element of public space by making the city a shared canvas. We believe that the people who use the city are the people that colour the city. We create inviting spaces that can be turned into valuable places by the users. Not just at certain points in time, but continuously. Below is a selection of WeTheCity's placemaking projects. If you're still hungry for more info after reading this, check out www.wethecity.nl.

BENCHESCOLLECTIVE

The gap between rich and poor, immigrants and locals, and low-skilled and highly educated people seems to be growing every year. Therefore, one of the most urgent challenges of our time is to combat structural inequality and promote mutual understanding. We believe that public space can play a vital role in this endeavour. This is what sparked the idea for the BenchesCollective.

The BenchesCollective is a platform that organises the biggest open-air café in the world. We encourage people to create a meeting place by adding a (permanent) bench on the sidewalk, preferably in front of their house. People can register their little café for a day on our website. Anyone can become part of the biggest open-air café or a local edition. As a host you can serve food and drinks, give salsa courses, play board games, set up a mini cinema, or organise music or anything else that makes you happy. Guests give a small donation or bring something

yummy themselves. This is how the BenchesCollective encourages people to invite and get to know their neighbours. Collectively, all of these new meeting places (spread across 17 countries) form a giant open-air café. As many as 2,500 people have already joined the BenchesCollective with over 1,350 benches in 17 countries bringing more than 20,000 people together. So transform your sidewalk and join the movement!

BOILING

As a city maker, there are a number of ways in which you can get funding for your (idealistic) initiatives. Municipalities and foundations are often your best bet. However, they require extensive project and budget plans, co-financers and take up a lot of your time. Boiling provides new possibilities for getting your project off the ground. It's fast, based on trust and relies on the power of the crowd.

Boiling is like an ammunition room for impatient city makers. Together, we determine the city's future, starting tomorrow. Anyone visiting a Boiling event donates €10 and gets a voting ballot and a simple dinner in return. During the first hour, four impatient city makers present their idea and tell the crowd what they need besides money. During the second hour, everybody enjoys their dinner and fills in their voting ballot, which consists of a voting point, a tipping point and a boiling point. You can vote, share tips, contacts, space and material, and even roll up your sleeves to help. The city maker with the most votes takes home all of the entrance fees, the amount of which is matched by an external party. All four city makers get a powerful piece of crowdsourced ammunition for their project. The only thing the winner needs to do in return is give a presentation at the next Boiling event. Boiling is currently active in Amsterdam and Rotterdam, and we are very much looking forward to taking the concept abroad.

PARK LIBRARY

Stress and obesity are both becoming increasingly prevalent problems in many cities around the world. The Parkotheek ('Park Library') promotes the better use of parks and celebrates a healthier lifestyle. Accordingly, we've created a demand-driven library for cool things you can use in parks, aiming to spark the imagination of their users and encourage them to explore all the different facets of parks.

Anyone can buy a membership card for the Park Library. Memberships is free for low-income families (who are especially afflicted by obesity). As a member, you get the opportunity to borrow cool things that you can share with fellow members. The Park Library community decides what will be added to the collection. It can be anything from trampolines and giant chessboards to guitars and soccer goals.

We offer businesses based near the park the opportunity to become sponsors. In return, all employees get a membership and the company can add three branded items to the library to create even more possibilities for enjoying the park.

The Park Library is a transformed cargo bike with a colourful storage container. In the future, it will have a building with a playful design based on a hay barn, the whole roof of which can go up when open. The Park Library is currently active in Noorderpark in Amsterdam. Since the collection is based on the ideas and the needs of the users, the concept is suitable for urban parks around the world.

ROEF

Currently, only 2% of the rooftop landscape in Amsterdam is being used. We want the remaining 98% to become green, sustainable and open to the public. This is why ROEF came about. It's a festival and symposium on the rooftops of 17 giant buildings in Amsterdam. All these buildings are spread around the Knowledge Mile, a field lab and BIZ (a company investment zone) that runs from Amstel Station to Waterlooplein. Besides impressive views, the festival consists of anything from binocular theatre shows to bird-based brass brands. Hosting a festival is not a goal but a means to show the potential of the vastly underused rooftop landscape.

The festival is based on rooftops that showcase a glass house, a farm, a swimming pool, solar panels, a smart roof, an edible vegetable garden, hot tubs and a sauna. By showing the festival's

diversity, we want people to be amazed by the potential opportunities offered by rooftops. That's the first step, which we call 'show'. The second step is to 'grow' the number of green, sustainable and public roofs. The symposium aims to bring together investors and rooftop pioneers in an inspiring way. The third step is to 'connect' rooftops with other rooftops and the ground level. The result will be an accessible skypark, generating much-needed tranquillity in the midst of hectic city life while making the city more green and sustainable.

ROEF is enjoying its third edition in Amsterdam, and Antwerp is excited to join. ROEF can be a perfect catalyst for the movement to make more use of the rooftop landscape in cities everywhere. Do you see a rooftop festival happening in your city?

TAKE ACTION
NOW

THE BUSINESS CASE FOR PLACEMAKING

Theo Stauttener, partner of Stadkwadraat

Placemaking injects new areas with new energy. During this process, city makers build new networks, and they're responsible for introducing new activities and ensuring that real estate and public places are used more effectively. The city maker optimises the use of the city. New activities, programmes and networks create value, not only in social and cultural terms but also from an economic and financial perspective.

Placemaking therefore has a proven added value to area development. It leads to better use, more activities, more participation, less vacancy, better rent prices for the owners in the area and a higher rate of return for the overall area. But it's important to develop a business case for placemaking to emphasise this added value and position placemaking solidly in area development.

CHANGES IN AREA DEVELOPMENT GENERATE A DIFFERENT APPROACH

Increasingly, area development is starting to signify the optimisation of our space. It concerns the better use of existing buildings and land, and adapting them by means of refurbishment, renovation and demolition/new-build.

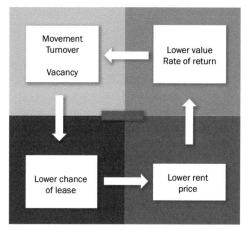
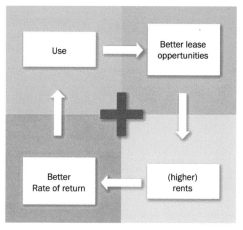

From downward to upward: The mechanism works two ways

These processes have shifted from drafting plans and stacking stones to coordinating demand, bringing together activities and generating new networks. Apart from the hardware that's already there (land and property), the software and orgware are becoming more and more important.

Area management has undergone substantial change as a result. Because the development of land and buildings initially became part of the business case as well, there was talk of postponement. Making housing more sustainable means investing more on the front-end, but it's precisely during development that this is recouped by means of lower energy costs. The management of the area has shifted more to the front-end because the development of existing buildings and land has become part of the area development.

THE INABILITY TO CAPTURE VALUE IS THREATENING PLACEMAKING

Initially, the development of existing areas doesn't necessarily focus on generating major cash flows. It's more about generating new programmes, events, activities and functions in a given area: in other words, placemaking. Functions are created with limited resources that, when successful, slowly but surely generate cash flow.

Placemaking makes a social, communal and cultural contribution to the area and provides it with new meaning. Increasingly, it's being organised based on new types of collectiveness in which parties work together and also share revenue.

In many areas, these collective activities disappear once the financial development of value takes off. More traditional types of building, property development and capital are replacing placemaking and conquering the area. As a result, all of the energy that has been pumped into these areas is being lost.

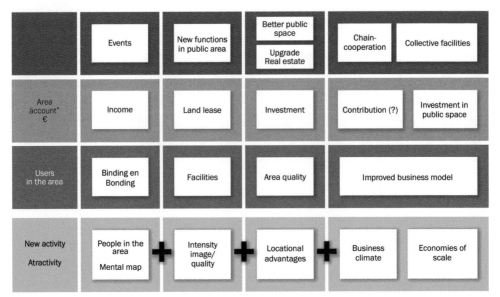

	Events	New functions in public area	Better public space / Upgrade Real estate	Chain-cooperation	Collective facilities
Area account" €	Income	Land lease	Investment	Contribution (?)	Investment in public space
Users in the area	Binding en Bonding	Facilities	Area quality	Improved business model	
New activity / Atractivity	People in the area / Mental map	Intensity image/ quality	Locational advantages	Business climate	Economies of scale

Place making and the rate of return of the area

Because the revenue from placemaking often falls into other people's hands, it remains difficult for city makers to invest, and therefore they amass little or no capital for ongoing or future projects. It's crucial for the healthy future of placemaking that value is distributed differently. This can only happen if city makers and placemakers adequately promote their added value. Recent developments suggest things are moving in the right direction.

THE HARD FACTS ABOUT THE PROPERTY MARKET: TRUST IN THE BASIS OF VALUE CREATION

The crisis in the land and property market has taught us important lessons. The devaluation of land and property was the consequence of a system in deadlock, but also of a loss of trust. This resulted in structural vacancy, falling returns, a deteriorating image of the areas, which set a downward spiral into motion.

The striking thing about this development is that it can be turned to the positive. Giving meaning to areas increases trust among residents, companies and investors, which galvanises a process of increased investment, less vacancy and an improved image. This is reflected in the fact that the area is increasing its output. More than anything else, the increased output is creating added value for the areas' economy, society and financial value.

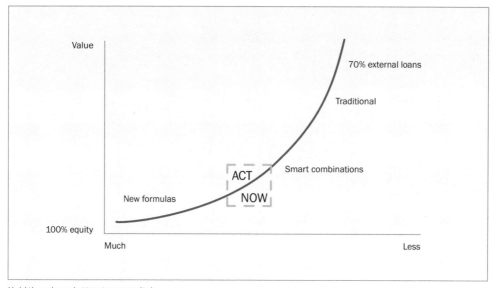

Value

70% external loans

Traditional

ACT
NOW

Smart combinations

New formulas

100% equity

Much

Less

Hold the grip and attract new capital

City makers and placemakers have proven themselves to be the engine that makes things happen. Now that the economic situation has improved and is enhancing growth and redevelopment, it's extremely important that these processes are also accorded a permanent position in area development. In terms of sustainability and housing construction, the task is so huge that it can't be handled only by city makers or traditional partners. This is a great opportunity for new area developers and the more traditional parties, who focus on construction, to forge partnerships. The question isn't whether we will opt for old or new area development, it's about which combination we decide to go for. In that sense, every task will be specifically defined and require a tailored approach. The programming has no choice but to give equal standing to placemaking and social and communal value creation, and a healthy business case for area transformation.

HIGHLIGHT THE ADDED VALUE

As far as that's concerned, the coming years will be interesting. That's when we can convert our placemaking experiences into new assignments, together with traditional real estate and area developers. For that to succeed, it's of crucial importance that we develop a business case for placemaking. Not only does it have to include financial and economic aspects, but also the added value for society and the community. That will make the

concept of 'value creation' real. And consequently the added value of placemaking will become visible so that it can be adequately acknowledged.

In addition to this business case, it's essential to generate new capital. For that to happen, new funds and other forms of funding, such as crowdfunding, have to be linked up with each other. These forms of funding provide people and companies with a much greater opportunity to invest directly in projects, areas and people that are meaningful to them. This is how they can become a partner in area development.

CITY AT EYE LEVEL IN NEW-BUILD PROJECTS

Mattijs van 't Hoff & Jeroen Laven (STIPO)

Many cities are developing new urban inner-city areas instead of suburban sprawl. These new areas (or the redevelopment of existing areas) have an urban look and feel: higher density, more amenities, a mix of housing types and other functions. What's most important for new urban areas is to create a pleasant city at eye level and a lively urban neighbourhood with good walkability.

However, not all new development areas in the Netherlands are succeeding in this aim. They lack diversity in terms of function, variety in architecture and/or good design of the plinths. The development of high density urban projects is complex, but it should always interact with the street at the ground floor level. Many projects seem to have lost sight of the human scale and experience. A pleasant experience at eye level depends on many aspects (Karssenberg et al., 2016), all which need to be taken into consideration while developing and designing these new areas.

Jane Jacobs' 1961 book *The Death and Life of Great American Cities* has demonstrated that there are four indispensable conditions when it comes to generating exuberant diversity in urban districts. First, there's the need for mixed use: more than one primary function. Second, blocks must be

Street without trees

Trees form a canopy in the street

short to create a fine urban grain in the street network with many corners. The third condition is the need for diversity in buildings, both in terms of age and condition. And four, sufficient density and concentration of people. Jan Gehl's *Close Encounters with Buildings*, published in 2006 has also provided us with many insights regarding life in between buildings, one of which is that the design of façades should appeal to pedestrians. Interesting façades have variety, multiple doors, visual contact and many functions.

Current new-build projects in the Netherlands reveal that creating a great city at eye level still faces challenges. An analysis of newly developed areas (or under development) in Amsterdam (Zuidas), Utrecht (Stationsgebied) and Rotterdam (Wijnhavenkwartier, Laan op Zuid, Katendrecht, and Nieuw Crooswijk) has provided us with new insights – which build on the knowledge of both Jane Jacobs and Jan Gehl's works. We found the following aspects to be important in creating a pleasant city at eye level.

DO 1: CREATE PLEASANT STREETS

Street width is important. Of course, this depends on the functional requirements and the hierarchy in the street network. However, some streets tend to become too wide, creating a feeling of emptiness and loneliness. For urban streets, a width of 13 to 20 metres seems to be just right for traffic, sidewalks, trees and a well-functioning hybrid zone. If a street is wider, a green zone should be added.

Trees are important for the character of a street. Every street should have trees on at least one of its sides and if possible on both. They function as a canopy for the street, creating a green atmosphere and providing protection against different kinds of weather (shade, for example). Trees also help to diminish the urban heat island effect and provide space for urban nature.

The sidewalk shouldn't be too narrow, nor should it be too wide, approximately 2.50 to 3.50 metres. Space for parking bicycles should be part of a functional zone on the sidewalk (together with space for trees, lamp posts and benches, for example), and not limit the width of the sidewalk. This functional zone is also a buffer between cars and pedestrians. If necessary and possible, parking for visitors along the sidewalk can be considered, but this shouldn't be the dominant feature of the street. Be careful not to park cars on the sidewalk because this can be unsafe for playing kids.

Sidewalk that's too wide

Sidewalk that's too narrow

The hybrid zone

DO 2: CREATE BLOCKS ON A HUMAN SCALE WITH A VARIETY OF USES

The size of the urban blocks should have a human scale, both in length and height. Small blocks create more variety in terms of the walking route with many corners for (neighbourhood) facilities. Urban blocks should also have a variety of units: something new every 5 to 7 metres. Many doors and entrances also create more opportunities for encounters and enhance the variety of the building. For future possible uses, urban blocks should have a flexible ground floor: physically (height at least 3.50 metres) but also in the zoning plan (residential, business and small-scale amenities). Corner units should be prioritised for adding special functions.

Ground floors must have active functions facing the street: shops, cafés, workspaces, kitchens and living rooms, for example. Dwellings and units on the ground floor also should have a separate front door to the street (not

Human scale architecture

Warm and tactile architecture

combined with entrances for apartments on other floors). A slight elevation of the ground floor (a maximum of 40 centimetres) can provide the right height for privacy for ground floor dwellings, while keeping eyes on the street. A hybrid zone (or façade garden) can also create privacy for ground floor dwellings, and they enhance ownership of the street.

DO 3: CREATE AN APPEALING PLINTH EXPERIENCE

The design and appearance of the ground floor should appeal to the pedestrian, something Jan Gehl calls the 5 km/h architecture. Both the functions and the architecture should be attractive and add to the walking experience by creating variety. Architecture should be warm and tactile (brick, brownstone or natural stone, for example) and have considerable detail. The design should not dominate either horizontally or vertically but have a great mixture of both, creating variety and maintaining a human scale while enhancing the overall cohesion of the architecture. Creating a variety of functions and uses in the plinth requires plinth management, such as in Amsterdam Zuidas. It needs a dedicated plinth manager to identify those functions that are missing and what's needed in the area, which will increase the use of the plinth.

The plinth should create a smooth transition from building to public space. The façade should have an openness, not by having lots of glass

Corner café

Mix of functions

Nice façade and window size

but rather a permeability between inside and outside. Big windows are undesirable as they either reflect and act as mirrors or violate the privacy of inhabitants and make them feel like they're living in an aquarium (thus causing them to close their windows with curtains or blinds). Creating smaller windows enhances people's feeling of privacy and provides space for more materialisation. Medical amenities such as doctor and dentist services tend to blind their windows for privacy reasons, creating dull façades. Instead they should only be allowed to have a reception desk and a waiting room on the street side.

The creation of a good city at eye level over the years is depends on the hardware, software and orgware:

- it depends on the design and quality of the streets, the buildings and the plinth itself;
- it depends on the functions and the use of the district, the street and the units; and
- it depends on the management and coalition of owners, entrepreneurs and inhabitants… to make it truly great.

THE SIDEWALK IS A LOGICAL PLACE TO MEET SOMEONE

Rehabilitating the Dutch sidewalk

Urban planner Eric van Ulden and urban psychologist Sander van der Ham are advocating the rehabilitation of the sidewalk as it was originally intended: as a buffer zone between public and private space. And please, let's just call it a sidewalk again. 'When you talk about hybrid or transition zones, no one really knows what you're talking about, even though we always had such a nice word for it.'

'A search for #stoep (which means sidewalk in Dutch, from which the English word stoop, a small porch, is derived) on Instagram mainly yielded hits with pictures of paving stones and dog turds,' says urban planner Eric van Ulden. 'But there was also a photo of US correspondent Erik Mouthaan who had used the hashtag #stoop in addition to #stoep. The former generated all kinds of beautiful pictures of the sidewalk as it had originally been in the Netherlands: a space of about 1.25 metres in front of the front door that belonged to the house. These 'stoops' also common in America, in the shape of a veranda or stairs leading to the front door. We now refer to sidewalks as transition zones, hybrid zones or as space in between. But actually no one has clue what you're talking about, even though we have such a nice word for it. Our mission is to bring back the sidewalk, as well as the meaning of the word, in its original definition.'

'But with a modern twist,' adds urban psychologist Sander van der Ham, 'so that the sidewalk in today's society can contribute to life on the street and to the communities in the neighbourhoods.'

In the Netherlands, the sidewalk goes back more than 500 years and was a buffer zone between houses and the carriages and the busy life on the street. Ironically, it vanished in the eighteenth century precisely because the cities became so much busier. The Dutch sidewalk made way for the French *trottoir*: a traffic-related space with an edge on the sidewalk that people could walk back and forth on. In 2011, Eric van Ulden and Daniel Heussen decided to research the function of the sidewalk. Because they definitely wanted to examine the social function of the sidewalk as well, they asked urban psychologist Sander van der Ham to join them. The research resulted in the publication of the book *De stoep. Ontmoetingen tussen huis en straat* ('The sidewalk: Encounters between house and street) in 2015.

'Apparently it's not possible to develop urban space in such a way that it's natural to meet each other,' Van der Ham says. 'It almost seems as if we need community centres or other organisations to get people to meet. And yet the sidewalk, a small space in front of your front door, can be a place where you casually meet the people that live around you.'

The Dutch research on sidewalks has confirmed the findings of Norwegian-Swedish research, which has shown that more than 80% of casual contact between neighbours takes place in transition zones. 'The people that use these transition zones have significantly more contact with their neighbours,' Van der Ham says. 'Not only do they chat more often in front of their door, but they also get together more often. Moreover, they're better at gauging their neighbours' lifestyle. Even leaning your bike on the façade helps. The fact that you spend a few moments there a couple of times a day has an enormous social function. So when you talk about the individualisation of society and about polarisation, the sidewalk could easily act as an important counterbalance to that. People strike up a conversation and talk about the weather, the street and whether it's a pleasant place to live. It's precisely these talks that make sure people get to know on another. The casual conversation as an antidote to individualisation in society.'

The research also revealed that as soon as something is placed on the sidewalk, it draws the gaze of passersby and causes them to look less inside, as a result of which residents feel freer. 'During our research we visited people in Blijdorp in Rotterdam that had nothing in front of their house,' Van Ulden says, 'so that passersby walked very close to the window. As it turns out,

the residents weren't making any use of the space bordering
the street. Their house had become like a museum, a "looking
house". I actually think that it's wrong to make people's houses
border directly onto the public domain. Just as we reserve a
certain amount of space for parking when we design, we should
do the same for the sidewalk when possible.'

'Not only does that make a street like that more pleasant,
but it's more pleasant for passersby too,' Van der Ham says.
'Anyone walking into a street with small front gardens
and pots and plants feels safer because it's visibly
a place that people care about.'

Luckily there are places where sidewalks are doing well. Such
as IJburg in Amsterdam, where one of these Dutch sidewalks
is part of the urban development plan. All architects and urban
planners are now obliged to incorporate that space in their
designs, and that has turned out well. And sidewalks are making
a comeback outside the Randstand conurbation too. The centre
of Groningen is deliberately returning the transition spaces to
residents. See also the chapter about Groningen on page 60.

There are few places where the difference between having a sidewalk or not is as clear as on Katendrecht in Rotterdam, where part of the apartment complexes on the quay has a small zone in front of the façade, whereas the other part does not. 'There's absolutely nothing going in the areas without that zone on the sidewalk,' Van der Ham says. 'People there keep their curtains closed and the public amenities there are turned inward. The people living in the area with small zone – simply a kind of strip placed in the sidewalk – have started using that space. And that has grown, in about three years' time, into a wealth of green.'

The plants also enhance the resilience of the city and its ability to adapt to climate change. 'Whereas we were initially interested in the social function,' Van Ulden says, 'now other developments are coinciding with the return of the sidewalk in front of the door. These transitions zones – sometimes just a little garden the size of a paving stone in front of the façade – provide space to insects such as bees. Because plants evaporate water and provide shade, they cool down the city, which is much warmer than the land surrounding it. The gardens also reduce the chance of flooding as they prevent all of the rainwater from going into the sewers.'

'The sidewalk turns out to be an important space in many parts of the city,' adds Van der Ham. 'Moreover, it's something that people really want. As a result, it spreads over the city like a web, initiated by the inhabitants themselves. That's really powerful.'

CLEANPICNIC: KEEP PARKS CLEAN WITH A PICNIC BLANKET

Thijs Verheugen was always the first one to sit in the park enjoying some refreshments, weather permitting. 'Great, but I also noticed that this generated a huge amount of antisocial litter, and it was getting worse every year. I could no longer bear it. Walking through the park it suddenly dawned on me: a picnic blanket on which to lay out your food, and once the picnic is over the blanket becomes a trash bag in one single operation. And that's it. Ideal because it makes tidying up easier and more fun. It's the simplest design I could think up together with Twan van Dommelen. A blanket with a hole through which the other three corners are pulled to create a trash bag. Hallelujah! The simpler, the better, and therefore also cheaper!'

'Trash bag and picnic blanket in one, ever so handy. Best thing in the world!' – Roos, Vondelpark visitor

PICNIC BLANKET AND TRASH BAG IN ONE

The design and the cheerful print are what make the CleanPicnic blanket such a success. The picnic pattern and the high user value make sure that visitors to the park are happy to receive and use the CleanPicnic blanket.

'We always take along a CleanPicnic blanket in the pram in case we go to a different park for a change, so we're always prepared.' – Joke, Sarphatipark visitor

CUSTOM MADE AND FREE

The concept much more than just the blanket. The CleanPicnic blankets are custom-made designs that are given to park visitors by local shopkeepers and park management free of charge. That way everyone helps to keep the backyards of our cities and villages clean.

'The widespread use of the picnic blankets means that we can reduce the number of men we need for clean-up work by two a day. That saves us 150,000 euros a year.' – Maurice Veldwachter, district manager at City District West (Westerpark)

TEST IN VONDELPARK

Verheugen had the idea in April 2010. In July he received the patent, and in August a test was launched in Vondelpark in collaboration with *Nederland Schoon* ('Clean Netherlands'). Peter Vos, park warden at the time, had not told his cleaning crew about the test. The following Monday they asked him where on earth all those trash bags in the waste containers came from. It had worked, and so they were given the green light.

'It makes people happy. The majority of visitors to Sarphatipark makes good use of the picnic blankets. The minority will follow suit.' – Riny Meijer, area management consultant for Public Space South (Sarphatipark)

STRUCTURAL SOLUTION

CleanPicnic does not sell blankets but it offers a structural solution for waste problems in parks. The concept's starting points are:

– Make cleaning up easier and more fun.
– Work together with visitors, local residents, neighbourhood shops and the park manager.
– Make it free for users.
– The cheerful look of the blankets encourages park visitors to clean up their own trash.
– Distribute the blankets directly to the picnicking public whenever possible to limit the amount of waste.

'A sign on the door points to the CleanPicnic blankets this year. I consider it a fixed element of the salad bar.' – Floris, Westerpark salad bar

SPECIFIC APPROACH

If a park has a litter problem and turns to CleanPicnic for help, we'll gather around the table to discuss this issue at length. Because every park is different and requires an individual approach. Some important questions have been raised, such as: what does the park look like, what kind of visitors does it attract, are hospitality options available, and are there sufficient trash cans in the park? Based on findings, CleanPicnic will present a proposal tailored to the park's situation. The proposal includes, among other things, the distribution network, the logistics involved in delivering the blankets, the trash bin locations, as well as promotion and publicity.

'It's not only sociable and fun, but it's also good to know that by using these blankets we keep the park clean; so it's a win-win situation.' – Paul Laudy, alderman at Public Space Leiden (Van der Werfpark)

THE ROLE OF PLACEMAKING

CleanPicnic works on the basis of the placemaking concept. This means that as many people as possible will be involved in the solution: park visitors, residents, neighbourhood shops, hospitality/park entrepreneurs, and park management. The solution and the key to success are in the hands of the people themselves and in a good partnership.

'Normally, we pay handsomely for cleaning work. Nowadays I look around and see practically nothing lying on the grass. Everything disappears in the picnic blankets, and suddenly it's gone.' – Bas Schreuder, organiser of Picnic Festival Leiden (Van der Werfpark)

SUCCESSFUL NEIGHBOURHOOD PROJECT

In the Vondelpark, CleanPicnic has developed into a successful neighbourhood project that brings together park visitors, local businesses, members of the community and park management. Everyone joins in, contributes and benefits. On summer days this year, visitors can pick up the iconic picnic blanket for their trash at one of 20 grocery shops or hospitality outlets in and around the Vondelpark. The Friends of the Vondelpark association is engaging volunteers to hand out the blankets. The Amsterdam municipality's park management department replenishes the stocks on summer days to ensure that sufficient trash blankets are always available for park visitors.

'We believe that by initiating the collaboration between park visitors, neighbourhood residents, local shopkeepers, hospitality outlets and park management we've found a positive answer to the Vondelpark's huge waste problem in recent years.' – Janine Geysen, Friends of the Vondelpark

RECYCLED PLASTIC AND PLANT MATERIAL

We purposely opted for producing the blankets in the Netherlands and not, for example, in China. This enables us to ensure that production is as sustainable as possible in all respects. There are two versions: blankets made of recycled plastic and of plant material, i.e. biobased. The blankets and the production process are in conformity with the Netherlands Commodities Act, which regulates food safety, among other things. This is important because people put their food on the blanket.

'It was obvious that the corners had to be pulled through the hole, so it serves as a trash bag that you can dispose of. Very handy.' – Yvonne, Van der Werfpark visitor

THE AIM

Meanwhile, CleanPicnic is helping to clean up parks in Amsterdam, Rotterdam, Dordrecht, The Hague, Groningen, Twente, Delft and Leiden. Consultations are also being held with other cities about the introduction of CleanPicnic, and partnerships have been established with Albert Heijn, ANWB and Mentos, to name a few. And there is a new initiative in the making: the CleanPicnic towel, a towel and trash bag in one, intended to also keep beaches clean. The aim is to launch the CleanPicnic towel in 2018.

CleanPicnic's mission is to offer a worldwide solution for litter in recreational areas by making cleaning up easy and fun. Much work remains to be done. All help is welcome.

'I thought right away: that's something we don't have in Ghent yet, so we should really launch this in Belgium too.' – Brecht, Sarphatipark visitor

HOW DO YOU MAKE A PLACE PLEASANT?

Kyra Kuitert ® RCE and Rosemarie Maas (Bureau KM)

Authors of *Prettige Plekken – Handboek Mens & Openbare Ruimte* ('Pleasant Places – Guide to Human Interaction with Public Space')

Everyone wants appealing public spaces in their city, whether you're a designer, politician or resident. In the Netherlands in any case, politics and policy focus strongly on participation, which means involving and listening to residents and users. Placemaking, which is now a global phenomenon, provides excellent guidelines in that sense. But participation doesn't lead, by definition, to the optimal use of public space. The latter also requires knowledge of the conditions for the good use of public space in the eyes of designers and planners.

What makes participation difficult is that those of the residents participating don' necessarily represent all of the inhabitants in a neighbourhood. After all, it requires quite some skill and time to acquaint yourself with the subject matter and express your opinion eloquently. Indeed, those who get involved in the plans often have a relatively high level of education or are vocal residents with a great deal of time on their hands. But not everyone has this much time to spare or the necessary skills.

Another drawback of participation is that it ends up being a 'compromise design': a mishmash of the sum of all desires, which often doesn't result in an attractive, pleasant place. A third problem with participation is that residents and designers sometimes view the desires and plans through different lenses. Does one group understand what the other one means by 'attractive' or 'child-friendly'? A different perspective can ultimately result in residents or users not getting the public space that they had in mind.

There's no doubt that participation is an indispensable part of the process towards creating good public space. But designers also need to have sufficient basic knowledge of what people consider to be pleasant public space. There appear to be many universal constants in that respect. Knowing and applying them should be at the foundation of designing public space.

Prettige Plekken – Handboek Mens & Openbare Ruimte, which was recently published in the Netherlands, provides a broad basis for this expertise. This guide came about based on the knowledge and experience of the authors, the studying of projects at home and abroad, an analysis of the literature on the subject and contributions by a diverse group of experts. The approximately 500 guidelines for the good use of public space are divided into the following themes: appeal, safety, easy to reach and easy to access, easy to move around in, social, child-friendly and green. What's more, the themes are accompanied by illustrations from more than 400 examples from all over the world.

Apart from providing these guidelines, the book also presents a clear vision of the spatial conditions that every public space should satisfy in order to qualify as a 'Pleasant Place'. These conditions are: Safety, Variation, Stay and Movement. If any of these four conditions is absent or has been given insufficient attention, then a place won't be perceived as being pleasant and therefore won't be used well.

Safety – It's important in public space that a sufficient number of people (whether consciously or not) keep an eye on things. Especially from their homes, because that helps to make public space safe as it creates the perception that people are present 24 hours a day.

Variation – The public space has to be attractive to look at, and there has to be sufficient variation, especially at eye level, such as detailed façades, art, water or green areas. If there's not enough to look at, people will get bored quickly and be gone before you know it.

Stay – If people have no place to sit they won't stay long. So there has to be a comfortable seating area (pleasant materials, preferably with backs and armrests) with a pleasant view of architecture, water or a green area, for example, but most importantly there has to be a view of people too. Watching people is the biggest attraction of public space. The place itself should be sheltered if possible from noise (such as traffic), weather and wind.

Movement – You have to be able to move quickly and easily from A to B by foot or by bike; the routes need to be logical, sufficiently wide and have a flat and hard underground so that they're also suitable for people in a wheelchair or walking with a pram. Recreational routes should be designed to run past water or green areas to the greatest extent possible and be connected to outdoor areas when feasible.

Artisplein Amsterdam

Leuvehoofd Rotterdam

Arena Boulevard Amsterdam

These four criteria show why the examples mentioned here are successful or not. Sometimes relatively minor interventions can turn a place around.

ARTISPLEIN AMSTERDAM

The free-standing chairs ensure that everyone can sit exactly the way they want to: in a group or alone, in the sun or in the shade. The ample green space provides variation and muffles the urban noise, as do the fountains. The walking route is wide enough and unimpeded.
The square borders a restaurant and is closed from 23:30 hrs onwards, so it's safe.

✔ Safe ✔ Stay ✔ Variation ✔ Movement

LEUVEHOOFD ROTTERDAM

This stony quay has been made green, and comfortable benches have been installed on the most attractive spot: in the sun, with a view of Erasmus Bridge. The location is full of variation: there's green, there's water and special architecture. The comfortable benches (made of wood with high backs) are located behind the walking route, so you can watch people walking by as well. There's no surveillance from homes here though, so it's potentially unsafe after dark.
Then again, there's no reason to come here at night anyway.

? Safe after dark ✔ Stay ✔ Variation ✔ Movement

ARENA BOULEVARD AMSTERDAM

There's enough light here at night for it to be safe after dark, but there aren't many eyes (informal surveillance) watching the square from buildings. You can't sit comfortably here. The seating edge is low and too hard. The square is also stony, and the long grey façade makes it look dull. More green would potentially soften the square.

✖ Safe after dark ✖ Stay ✖ Variation ✔ Movement

REFLECTIONS

PLACEMAKING AND THE DISCOURSE OF THE PUBLIC PLACE

Wouter Jan Verheul (Delft University of Technology)

The importance of pleasant public spaces in the city cannot be overstated. It's astonishing to see how much appeal a pleasant place can have on us as city dwellers, as daily users, as tourists or as random passers-by. We like to be surprised by a beautiful park or square, where we can relax in the green outdoors or look at the people around us. We prefer to walk or cycle the long way through a pleasant street with varied façades and a mixed use of the plinth than go through a dull or unpleasant street.

Good public space gives an area identity. It tells the story of a place, encourages encounters or offers other potential uses of a place that suit our specific need at that moment. It contributes to economic prosperity, to safety, health and happiness (Jacobs, 1960). Creating or improving public space is therefore a challenging task for anyone whose work is related to the city: from social workers to property developers, from architects to city marketers.

A focus on public space is not a given, however. Too often, public space is still neglected by administrators, designers and developers of the built environment. Either that, or it's under threat from (creeping) external developments such as safety, control, efficiency or commerce. We can therefore ask ourselves: What makes our space public? What makes public

space attractive? And how can we ensure that an attract place endures? To answer these questions, we need to consider the meaning of public space, the different types of interventions that can create or improve (placemaking) public space and, finally, how to set an agenda for placemaking.

PUBLIC SPACE IN THREE DISCOURSES

The reflections and discussions on public space differ substantially. As a result, public space is designed and managed in different ways. A discourse is a coherent entity of language, words, symbols and forms that steer the way we think and act. When it comes to public space, we can distinguish between at least three influential discourses: public space as a *free meeting space*, public space as a *frictionless transition space* and public space as a *theme-driven consumption space*.

The discourse of public space as a *free meeting space* is the classic ideal of a place that's truly public: it's a place by and for everyone. That means that the public space in a heterogeneous society has a variety of users. The public space is a communal (civil society) gathering space (agora). In this discourse, it concerns meeting, exchanging, getting to know people, forming ideas, and therefore also democracy (see Habermas, 1962;

Hajer and Reijndorp, 2001). There are manifestations of this discourse throughout history. Think of the market square in the Greek polis, Vienna's coffee houses or English parks, such as Hyde Park with its speakers' corner as concrete examples of public space belonging to all people and free speech. These days, local policy aims to use public space in neighbourhoods to get people out of their private domain and in touch with other people. City makers' plans also frequently focus on the quality of the public space as a place to spend time and meet other people.

Public space as a free meeting space is at odds with another discourse: public space as a *frictionless transition space*. This discourse is about management and control, efficiency and safety. The aim of modernist urban development is mainly to create tidier cities by building straight streets, dividing the functions of living, working and recreation, and providing much space for cars. And all that preferably in a build environment with a great deal of uniformity and predictability. For decades, Le Corbusier influenced urban planners with his notions of the city as an ordered machine – in which the street has no other function than connecting A to B, seeing as 'Man walks in a straight line because he has a goal and knows where he is going' (Le Corbusier, 1929). This discourse is reflected in many work locations, in and around stations or in shopping centres. On top of that, the culture of fear, safety and control has introduced the use of CCTV cameras, public transport gates and the lack of green areas, because the space is meant for transition, and friction between people has to be prevented (Garland, 2000). Presumably the persistent fear of terrorist attacks will not alleviate this fear anytime soon.

Another discourse that limits potential places as free meeting space is that of the *theme-driven consumption space*. Public space in this discourse is the place where users are mainly consumers that need to be entertained and from whom you must make a profit. As a result of globalisation, retail chains and hospitality formulas appear in the same form everywhere. The city has become a theme park (Sorkin, 1992). Tourists are seduced by spectacles in the shape of extravagant icon architecture (the landmarketing of the city) with the requisite souvenirs in tourist shops (Verheul, 2012). An extreme example of theme-driven consumption space is Times Square in New York, with actors in Disney character suits in a décor of international brands screaming at us from screens. But the centre of Amsterdam is also an example, where local trade is increasingly being replaced by waffle and Nutella shops. The small, non-touristic towns and villages are also succumbing to McDonaldization (Ritzer, 1996).

PLACEMAKING AS THE RECLAMATION OF SPACE

The above-mentioned developments and influences from the outside reveal that many places are losing their public and local character. Modernisation, globalisation and commercialisation are to blame. 'Places are turning into everywhere else' (Zukin, 2010) and are thus actually becoming a 'non-place' (Augé, 1992). Places are appearing where we don't feel at home, where we want to move through as quickly as possible, or even avoid – sometimes with negative consequences for the city or surrounding areas.

The question is what we can do to give the places a public identity. A variety of examples of placemaking show that places are never lost. Places can be revived in relatively simple ways and with few resources, be embraced by a diverse public and even have all kinds of positive spillover effects on adjacent places.

What are the various forms and function of placemaking? *Cultural placemaking* is perhaps the clearest form of placemaking in which a place is given new identity. Think, for example, of performances by local musicians, of theatre and of sports activities. The Schouwburgplein in Rotterdam, which used to be mainly empty and draughty, has been given a facelift together with cultural institutions. It is particularly when cultural placemaking is in synch with local character that it can help stop a place from becoming alienated.

Economic placemaking concerns increasing the value of a place and its surroundings. There are many examples of vacant areas where temporary or permanent initiatives have pulled a place out of a negative spiral of deterioration. A classic example is Bryant Park in New York, where property owners from the area invested in the park through a company investment zone. They, in turn, were responsible for a positive development in the value of property. In Nieuwegein, an area cooperative consisting of various partners was set up for an unattractive office location. They discovered what was wrong with the place and what was missing through an area evaluation (placegame). In the meantime, interest in the location has grown immensely, resulting in rising property prices.

A variation of economic placemaking is *innovative placemaking*. The idea is that a diversity of people with their own knowledge and competences will lead to new innovations and that the public space there will play a major role in this. The assumption is that cafeterias and public workplaces will be a key facilitator in this process. The municipality of The Hague is currently working with the business community and higher education on the so-called Central Innovation District in order to develop a high-quality knowledge industry. Together with the American Brooking Institution (the Bass Center), Project for Public Spaces and the Delft University of Technology they're attempting to discover exactly what is needed in public places to encourage cross-sector cooperation and new innovations.

Whereas economic and innovative placemaking mainly focus on the city's economic prosperity, *social placemaking* focuses on social tasks. It concerns placemaking that focuses on community building, on bringing people into contact with each other, on helping people with their needs and on bringing them out of social isolation. A unique example is how Bakery De Eenvoud in Amsterdam moves into neighbourhoods to bake bread with people. The act of baking (kneading, baking and eating) is a low-threshold one and helps people to talk about their concerns, sometimes with an openness not reserved for formal care institutions.

PLACEMAKING AS A MULTI-STAGE PROCESS

It's important that we don't view placemaking too narrowly as a single activity. Placemaking consists of different functions (as described above) and it often involves multiple interventions. We can distinguish between four types of intervention: the *hardware*, the *software*, the *mindware* and the *orgware* of placemaking. Because there is a great deal of linguistic confusion about what we understand placemaking to mean, it would be useful to define it and illustrate it more clearly.

The *hardware of placemaking* is about making a concrete physical intervention in public space. Today there is much knowledge available about the criteria that attractive public space has to meet. There are guides by William Whyte (1980), Allan Jacobs (1993) and Jan Gehl (2010) containing a great deal of useful advice about the dos and the don'ts of squares, streets, parks and the plinths of buildings. The common thread is the idea that we must take the users' expertise seriously and, as Jan Gehl suggests, 'experience the city at eye level and at five kilometres an hour.' Among other things, that means more space for pedestrians, wider sidewalks, no blind plinths, but a varied and open ground floor, with a mixed function, varied architecture, cosy squares and the opportunity to sit and seek shelter.

The principles of a well-designed space may sound logical, but they're definitely not known to all designers or developers. Blind walls or mirrored windows are still a common sight along new streets, and there are still many large, empty squares. 'If in doubt, leave some meters out', is Gehl's advice (Gehl, 2010). Riverfronts in many cities are barely being used: public space is absent and buildings have been built with their backs to the water.

The *software of placemaking* concerns programming and activities in public space. In Almere, for example, a desolate square in the city centre has been changed by organising beach volleyball, live music and cooking workshops. We can achieve a great deal by designing public space well, but interventions in the *hardware* are usually not sufficient on their own, sometimes too complicated or simply too expensive. The American organisation Project for Public Spaces (PPS) has shown through their 'lighter, quicker, cheaper' approach that by organising a few activities, public space will be used differently. In the Netherlands the BenchesCollective is trying to entice people to put benches on sidewalks, parks and squares on certain days of the week, thereby creating a major open-air café.

If a public place really wants to be actively used by a diverse public, then you have to be able to do multiple things there. According to environmental psychology, people are happiest when they use a place that is consistent with their own needs. For one person that means sitting and watching people, for another it means playing a ball game and for yet another it means peacefully daydreaming. That's why PPS uses the rule of 'the power of ten': there have to be at least ten reasons why people will use the public space.

The *mindware of placemaking* concerns how placemaking alters the way that we look at places. In Breda, the 'Via Breda' programme, in and around the station, has changed the way people experience the two city districts on opposite sides of the railway tracks. Placemaking can completely change how people view places, particularly desolate places and fringe areas. The Zomerhofkwartier in Rotterdam, for example, was an unknown, uninteresting area on the edge of the centre that people usually avoided. Public developer STIPO, together with housing association Havensteder and other partners, invested for years in different types of placemaking, and as a result the area has improved in every respect.

The *orgware of placemaking* concerns the partners in question, their mutual cooperation and how they organise themselves. Established institutions are increasingly adapting their traditional top-down role. It's no longer the administrator, project developer or designer that knows, from the vantage point of their meeting room or drawing table, exactly what needs to happen to a place – rather, the 'community is the expert'. That means deciding with local users what needs to change or what can be improved, how institutions incorporate these findings in their redesign and what kind of initiatives a city's inhabitants can develop themselves. In De Binckhorst in The Hague, BPD discovered that instead of first developing an all-encompassing masterplan, it was better off to start by organising minor activities with other parties to change the area. Indeed, at the outset there was no clear picture of what kind of property development would take place. In Dordrecht, the municipality had to accept a supervisory role in a place maintained by residents and manage expectations by explaining to users what the municipality can and cannot do.

Ogware also concerns the people behind the success of an initiative. Frequently activities depend on several enthusiastic people, which can be a vulnerable situation to be in. Sustainable initiatives in public space generally rely on a broad network with multiple nodes (Könst, 2017).

CHALLENGES FOR MAINTAINING PLACEMAKING

Even though many places are bereft of their local character, their quality as a place to spend time or their public value, places are never hopeless. The practice of placemaking has already generated many impressive examples of improved places. Of course, prevention is better than cure: clients, designers and developers should view users as experts from the start and put public value high on the agenda. In doing so, they can allow themselves to be led by guides on how to design attractive public space. But even if this is *not* done from the very start, placemaking can bring about changes for the good. To achieve this, city makers and researchers of public space and placemaking have to deal with a number of challenges.

Initiatives for placemaking would do well to study, demonstrate more effectively and showcase their added value. Now that the economic crisis is over, there is more pressure to develop properties quickly. Sometimes that also means that international financers and developers, who are far removed from local practices, may overlook local users. Whereas local initiatives were an effective way of preventing vacant areas from further deteriorating during the economic crisis, the pressure on space is so immense now in some places, that civil society parties are not even considered anymore. Luckily there are examples of prime locations where owners realise that you shouldn't always go for the highest bidder and that it's important to retain existing, low-threshold functions in the area. But that's certainly not the case everywhere. City makers will have to demonstrate the added value of their initiatives, and that will require more systematic research than the anecdotal evidence which the world of placemaking too frequently limits itself to currently.

City makers would do well to continue to base their initiatives on the essence of the ideal of public space as a place for a heterogeneous group of users. Sometimes initiatives are in danger of falling prey to their own success, or an enthusiastic group of permanent users is unaware of how their use of a place can restrict other type of use. For example, that could mean that in addition to noisy activities there also has to be space for silence, for people who don't wish to participate in a joint activity but want to quietly read a book. For some people public space is a place where you can take off your shoes, but perhaps that's not everyone's cup of tea. Nor is everyone always in the mood to actively meet people. So, to phrase the question as a paradox: how can you also create some privacy in public space? There is never a strict division of the public and the private: we discover pieces of the private in public space, just as we do pieces of the public in the private domain (Van Melik, 2008). The question is how to organise this alternation at the urban and neighbourhood level in such a way that justice is done to the diversity of society.

Looking for diversity in placemaking also means asking yourself which people or groups are not represented during public meetings or in the co-creation of a place. That could mean people with low or people with high levels of education, the elderly or youth, volunteers or businesspeople. Initiators and managers of public space have to be aware that activities can have the effect of both welcoming and excluding people.

Initiatives in public space require checks and balances and an equilibrium in the triangular relationship between the government, the business community and civil society. The government, for example, can establish rules and maintain order by means of its traditional (constitutional) position and democratically elected authority, but it can also play a facilitating role by providing parties with process supervision. The business community, on the other hand, is mainly familiar with market stimuli: it knows how to satisfy consumers and develop healthy business models. Involved citizens are part of civil society. They aim to set up activities with each other based on trust and enthusiasm, which is not always feasible in an anonymous relationship with the government or the business relationship with the market. All three sides of the triangle have their strong and weak points, and it's important to be aware of how to best incorporate each of these placemaking initiatives into this triangle.

Placemaking is never finished. There are still hundreds of places that need placemaking. Think, for example, of all the small and medium-sized station areas that have not been dealt with in recent years, in contrast to the large stations. Also think of the riverfronts or obsolete vacant industrial estates. Or think, on the other hand, of shiny new projects, where too much attention was devoted to façades by starchitects and too little on the public space around them. There's still plenty to do when it comes to placemaking, and we learn from past mistakes and successes. As soon as we reduce placemaking to a stunt or a formula that can be applied everywhere, then we're failing to appreciate the individuality and dynamics of time and space. The art is to continue innovating. Only then can a variety of users feel connected to a place and really feel at home there.

APPENDIX

ABOUT THE CONTRIBUTORS

This book is made possible by the following municipalities and organizations in the Netherlands, who were so kind to share their own Dutch examples on the city at eye level.

THE URBAN SCALE

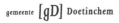

AREA DEVELOPMENT

BIBLIOGRAPHY

City at Eye Level in New-build Projects, pg. 209-217:
J. Jacobs (1961), The Death and Life of Great American Cities.
Gehl, J. (2006), Close Encounters with Buildings.
Karssenberg, H. et al. (2016), The City at Eye Level.
de Nijs, M. (2015), Highrise op ooghoogte (Highrise at eye level).

How do you make a place pleasant?, pg. 228-231:
Prettige Plekken – Handboek Mens & Openbare Ruimte
www.prettigeplekken.nl (viewing copy in English)
Bureau KM – Advice on Using Public Space
www.bureaukm.nl / info@bureaukm.nl

Placemaking and the discourse of the public place, pg. 234-243:
Auge, M. (1995) Non-places. Introduction to an anthropology of supermodernity. New York: Verso Books.
Corbusier, C.E. Le (1929; 1971) The City of Tomorrow and its Planning. London: Architectural Press.
Garland, D. (2000) The Culture of Control. Crime and Social Order in Contemporary Society. Chicago: The University of Chicago Press.
Gehl, J. (2010) Cities for People. Washington: Island Press.
Habermas, J. (1962; 1982) The Structural Transformation of the Public Sphere. Cambridge: Polity.
Hajer, M. and Reijndorp, A. (2001) In Search of New Public Domain. Analysis and Strategy. Rotterdam: NAi Press.
Jacobs, J. (1960) The Life and Death of Great American Cities. New York: Random House.

Jacobs, A. B. (1993) Great Streets. Cambridge: MIT Press.
Könst, A. (2017) Privaat beheer van de openbare ruimte. Benodigde condities voor het beheer van buurttuinen door bewoners. Rotterdam: Erasmus University Rotterdam / MCD.
Melik, R. van (2008) Changing Public Space: the Recent Redevelopment of Dutch City Squares. Utrecht: Utrecht University.
Ritzer, G. (1996) The McDonalidization of Society. An Investigation into the Changing Character of Contemporary Social Life. Thousand Oaks: Pine Forge Press.
Sorkin, M. (ed.) (1992) Variations on the Theme Park. The New American City and the End of Public Space. New York: Hill and Wang.
Verheul, W.J. (2012) Stedelijke iconen. Het ontstaan van beeldbepalende projecten tussen betoog en beton. The Hague: BoomLemma.
Verheul, W.J. (2015) Plaatsgebonden identiteit: het anker voor stedelijke ontwikkeling. In: Hafkamp et al. De Stad kennen, de stad maken. Kennis voor krachtige steden. The Hague: Platform31.
Whyte, W.H. (1980) The Social Life of Small Urban Spaces. New York: PPS.
Zukin, S. (2010) The Naked City. The Life and Death of Authentic Urban Places. Oxford: Oxford University Press.

PHOTO CREDITS

Photos and images with the articles are provided by the corresponding author(s) / interviewee(s) or STIPO, unless otherwise stated below.

Photos and images with the articles are provided by the corresponding author(s) / interviewee(s) or STIPO, unless otherwise stated below:

Towards place-led development in the porous city, pg. 14: by Iris Vetter, pg.15 top: by Tom Baas, pg. 15 bottom: by STIPO, pg. 17: by Lotte de Graaf

Placemaking has to go beyond being temporary, pg. 24: by STIPO, pg. 25 top: by Ethan Kent, pg. 25 bottom: by Michiel Landeweerd

Public space and placemaking in NL, pg. 32: by STIPO, pg. 33 top: by Gergo Hevesi, pg 33 bottom: by Ethan Kent, pg. 37, 39 and 41: by STIPO, pg. 40: by Gergo Hevesi

Placemaking + Friesland = mienskip, pg. 46 bottom: by Gemeente Leeuwarden

Drechtsteden: working on a Drierivierenpunt with no internal borders, pg. 52 bottom: by BGSV

Main shopping area in Tilburg: Working together to build a great city, pg. 56-58: by Jostijn Ligtvoet

Doing it together simply results in a better plan, pg. 62: by LOLA Landscape Architects, pg. 63 and 64: by Gemeente Groningen

Koekamp, linking the city and the woods, pg. 67: by DELVA Landscape Architects ; Urbanism, pg. 69 and 70: by Gemeente Den Haag

Maastricht: placemaking is a lengthy process, pg. 78 and 79: by Gemeente Maastricht

Inner City Plan of Attack: how Doetinchem is giving the inner city back to residents and entrepreneurs, pg. 85-87: by Gemeente Doetinchem

An urban living room six minutes from Schiphol Airport, pg. 94 bottom: by STIPO, pg. 95: by M. van der Heide, pg. 96: by Naigel Vermeulen

Spoorzone Delft, a new space in a historic city centre, pg. 98, 100 and 102: by Gemeente Delft, pg. 100 top: Jannes Linders

Transformation of station area turns Breda into hip and vibrant city, pg. 106: by Via Breda, pg. 107 and 108 bottom: by Gemeente Breda, pg. 108 top: by Rene de Wit

The metamorphosis of Sloterdijk, pg. 111-114: by E. van Eis

Spoorzone Tilburg: in the footsteps of the king and queen, pg. 118 top: by Jostijn Ligtvoet, pg. 118 bottom: by Gemeente Tilburg, pg. 119: by Willie-Jan Staps

As an area developer, we facilitate placemaking, pg. 121 and 122 top: by ANNA Vastgoed & Cultuur, pg. 122 bottom: Suzanne Monnier, pg. 124: by Arthur van der Lee - Woonpioniers

Club Rhijnhuizen is the perfect example of making your own luck, pg. 127-130: by Club Rhijnhuizen

Placemakers in Arnhem search for (and find) **Rhinegold**, pg. 137-140: by Gemeente Arnhem

Everyone can claim their own spot, pg. 144: by Robin Bakker

The Association has made it possible to achieve the impossible. That makes you greedy, pg. 156 top: by Joke Schot & Vereniging Verenigd Schouwburgplein, pg. 156 middle: by Eric Fecken, pg. 156 bottom: by Emine Yalcinkaya

The refreshing wit of the Honig complex, pg. 162: by Thea van den Heuvel, pg. 163 top: by Marieke Kramer, pg. 163 bottom and 164: by Roy Soetekauw

Joint vision of a beach on the Zaan, pg. 169: by Simone Ronchetti, pg. 170: by Rick Meijer

The Belfort Square in Almere: from a bleak square to a booming restaurant hub, pg. 175: by Geert van der Wijk

Harvesting the incentive for a great ZOHO at eye level, pg. 178-181: by Dahlia Soliman

Open-air Hotel Van Schaffelaar: sleeping beneath more than four stars, pg. 183 and 185 top: by Iris Vetter, pg. 185 bottom and 186: by Lex de Jong

WeTheCity: from boiling events to the world's biggest open-air café, pg. 198: by Tom Baas for BenchesCollective, pg. 200 top and bottom: by BenchesCollective, pg. 201: by Niki Boomkens

The business case for placemaking, pg. 205-208: by Stadkwadraat

City at Eye Level in New-build Projects, pg. 209-217: by STIPO

The sidewalk is a logical place to meet someone, pg. 219 top: by STIPO, pg. 219 bottom: by Daniel Heussen, pg. 221: by Eric van Ulden

How do you make a place pleasant?, pg. 230 top and bottom: by Kyra Kuitert (Bureau KM), pg. 230 middle: by Rosemarie Maas (Bureau KM)

Placemaking and the discourse of the public space, pg. 237: by STIPO

ACKNOWLEDGEMENT

The history of the City at Eye Level network begins in Rotterdam. In 2011 the municipality of Rotterdam asked STIPO to help it develop an approach to the plinths in the city centre. We started by setting up three pilot projects and concluded by developing a plinth strategy for the entire city centre.

Developing a plinth strategy for Rotterdam caused a mild form of professional deformation. Suddenly, everywhere we looked we saw poor plinths and ways of improving them. At the same time, by looking around us we discovered many inspiring examples of good plinths all over the world. This was sufficient reason for us to start working on our first 'City at Eye Level' book, which in the meantime has grown into a 'City at Eye Level' series and an international network. It has turned out to be a source of inspiration for people working on good plinths and public spaces.

During the time that we published our book and as the 'City at Eye level' network has grown, so has international attention for the importance of public space and plinths. In the meantime, STIPO has visited many cities in different countries to talk about the subject, and we work with various local partners to create better places in their cities. In 2016 we published a second edition of The City at Eye Level containing yet more stories from all over the world. We're also working on a book called 'The City at Eye Level for Kids'. Finally, we have launched an international City at Eye Level training course that has attracted participants from various continents.

We're extremely grateful to have as partners the Project for Public Spaces, Pakhuis de Zwijger and Placemaking Plus, with whom we organised Placemaking Week 2017

in Amsterdam. The latter was an opportunity for the international community that's working on a good city at eye level to convene in order to share the latest insights and examine how we can strengthen our cities.

The Placemaking Week prompted us to compile this book. It's a compilation of current examples of Dutch municipalities, developers, cultural partners, financial experts, advisors and other initiators who are working on a good city at eye level. We're grateful that many of these partners were enthusiastic about developing this book with us. It would have been impossible to create this book without their involvement and contributions. We hope that this book will not only show the international community what's happening in the Netherlands, but that it will also generate mutual inspiration and cooperation within the Netherlands. That's why we think it's great that this book is being published both in English and Dutch.

We're grateful for the willingness of dozens of professionals who have shared their stories with us, thus making this Dutch book possible. It was a *tour de force* to get to talk to all of these professionals during the summer holidays. Indeed, they took special pains to free up time for us. We're pleased and surprised by the openness of their stories: they not only shared their successes with us but also their quests and at times failures. Thanks to this openness, the book gives us unique insight into all of the efforts to improve the city at eye level. These stories could never have been written with such sparkling prose, nor so quickly, without the journalistic expertise of Menno Bosma, Maaike de Hon and Edith van Ewijk from 'Wereld in Woorden'. Thanks to Mark Speer's translations we can publish the book both in English and Dutch.

This book would never have looked so beautiful without the dedication of multi-talented designer and architect Paola Faoro in Boston.

Finally, we're grateful for the cooperation throughout the years of all the professionals that we encountered while working on the City at Eye Level; Meredith Glaser, Mattijs van 't Hoff and Jan van Teeffelen, who embarked on the City at Eye Level adventure with us from the start; and our colleagues at STIPO and the STIPO network, who continuously help to strive to link the work of The City at Eye Level to other ways of strengthening the city.

Jeroen Laven, Sander van der Ham, Sienna Veelders and Hans Karssenberg, STIPO.